Hawks on High

Everyday Miracles in a Hawk Ridge Season

Savage PRESS
14172 E Carlson Rd. • Brule, WI 54820
(218) 391-3070 • www.savpress.com

Hawks on High

Everyday Miracles in a Hawk Ridge Season

~ poems ~
Phil Fitzpatrick

~ drawings ~
penny perry

First Edition

Copyright 2019

All rights reserved.

Cover Design: penny perry

No part of this book may be reproduced in any form or by any electronic or mechanical means including information storage and retrieval systems without permission in writing from the publisher, excepting for short excerpts in a public review.

ISBN: 978-1-937706-22-7

Library of Congress Catalog Number: 2019932899
Published by: Savage Press 14172 E Carlson Rd. Brule, WI 54820

Savage PRESS

14172 E Carlson Rd. • Brule, WI 54820
(218) 391-3070 • www.savpress.com

Email: mail@savpress.com
Website: www.savpress.com

Contact the author at: fitztrick@gmail.com
Contact the artist at: perryframing@aol.com
Printed in the United States of America

To Elizabeth Converse Hunter,

and in memory of

Persis and Joe Fitzpatrick

Contents

Foreword

Preface

    In the Beginning — 12

The Place and Its People — 13
    Perfect Duluth Day — 14
    Oracular Info — 15
    Plumology — 16
    Lesson — 17
    Clinton — 19
    Wizardry — 20
    Streaming — 21
    Pringles Prize — 22
    Legend — 23
    The Uninvited Guest — 24
    You Can Have It Both Ways — 25
    Redtail Release — 26
    Kaitlyn's Wow — 27
    Tarsometatarsus — 28
    High-Interest Loan — 29
    Everybody's an Expert — 30

Of Time, Space and History — 31
    Hawks on High — 32
    That Old Gang of Mine — 33
    But Who's Counting — 34
    Extinction Event — 35
    Rhetorical Question — 36
    Dead Hawks — 37
    Surmising — 38
    Hawk Eye — 39
    Kettle — 40
    Ghost Birds — 41
    Whiteness, for Instance — 42
    Headset Hawk — 43
    The How of It — 44
    First Migrant — 45
    Black on Gray — 46

Dramatis Personae — 47
    Peregrine Over Hawk Ridge — 48
    Black Quintet — 49
    Little Blue Darter, or the Aha Moment — 50
    Parallax — 51

Harrier Brown	52
Double Gos Tease	53
Tee Vee	54
Better Late Than Later	56
The Big One	57
Ingrid, the Lapland Longspur	58
Miracle Missed	59
One Hundred Fifty Mya	60
Jack	61
Declension	62

For the Nestlings — 63
- Geography Lesson — 64
- Flying Ichabods — 65
- Now Playing Right Field — 66
- Tweet, Chip, Meow — 68
- A Day on My Rock — 69
- The Falcon Box — 70

A Quartet of Quartets — 71
Falco Peregrinus
- Peregrine Cam — 72
- Cam Medley — 73
- First Flight — 74
- Gone, But . . . — 75

Full Disclosure
- First Day — 76
- Forget the Binos! — 77
- Chevron Wings — 78
- Just Specks — 79

I Shall Be Released
- Release I — 80
- Release II — 81
- Release III — 82
- Andy and the Sharpie — 83

All Things Must Pass
- Perspective — 84
- The Season's Last Bald — 85
- Closing Time — 86
- November — 87

Glossary — 88

Acknowledgments — 89

Bibliography — 91

Other Poems About Hawks — 92

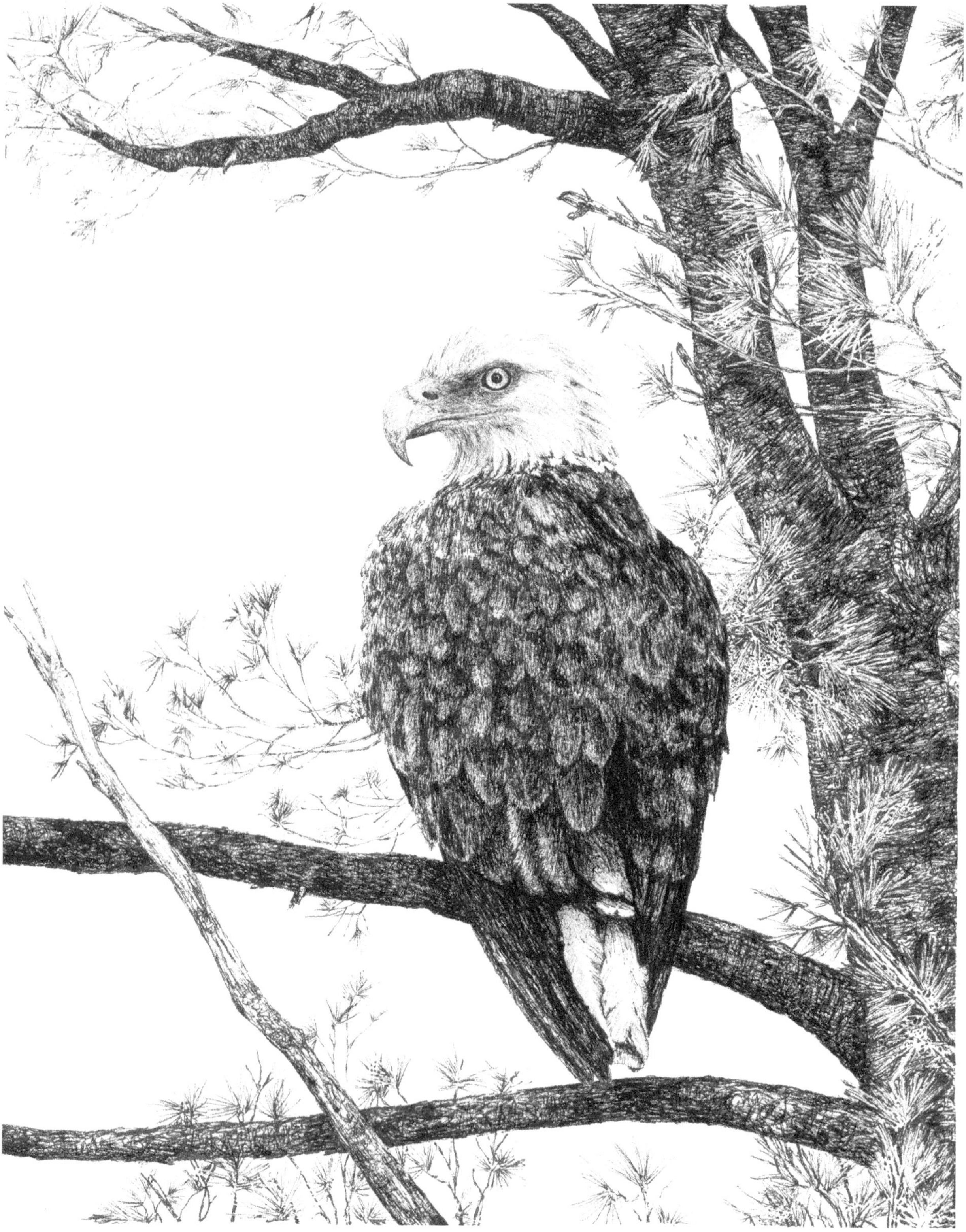

Foreword

Phil Fitzpatrick's lifelong rapture for all things raptorial shows no signs of abating. It waxes stronger with each of the poems he wrote for Hawks on High: Everyday Miracles in a Hawk Ridge Season. What is most lovely about this collection—a kettle containing about 70 individual titles Fitzpatrick composed over a two-year period—is the gently humorous way he entwines the majesty of the hawks during their fall migration with the devotion of watchers bringing various degrees of patience and expertise. Fitzpatrick's eye is sharp when it catches the glint in an eagle's eye and gently amused by the fumbling and mumbling of the rookie birder. The Everyday Miracles are not only these remarkable birds soaring overhead, but the people who strain their necks to see them. These poems are the interface between wild masters of the sky and the ones stuck on the cold ground. They portray humanity's place in the wild. We are fortunate that the community which autumnally coalesces on a windswept Minnesota ridge near Duluth has been so touchingly rendered by Phil Fitzpatrick's words, matched by artist Penny Perry's elegant lines in pen and ink.

And don't miss the glossary at the back.

Dyana Z. Furmansky

Preface

I must have been channeling Wordsworth the day I decided to write this book. His conviction that poetry is nothing more, nothing less than "the spontaneous overflow of powerful feelings" exactly fits how I was feeling the day a Peregrine Falcon zoomed over my head and down past the tree tops the first time I visited Hawk Ridge. That was in the fall of 2017. There followed two Hawk Ridge seasons of powerful feelings, the overflow of which you now hold in your hands.

But let's keep it simple: plainly, I'm trying to do the impossible here. I am trying to make tangible something that is inherently intangible. The phenomenon of bird migration—and it is every bit a phenomenon—happens the world over. It goes on constantly, and it is constantly changing. There are people all over the world, scientists and nonscientists alike, who spend a good deal of their time studying it. We know quite a bit about migration now thanks to them, but there is still something about it that remains ineffable, mysterious and endlessly fascinating to us. That intangible "something" captivates hundreds of thousands of people every autumn across the country and, indeed, around the world at raptor counting sites.

The migration of raptors is a very small fraction of all bird migration even though there are hundreds of sites in North America alone where people watch and count migrating raptors. Despite being one of the most renowned of these sites ("undeniably world class" in the words of Duluth's first Poet Laureate, Bart Sutter), Hawk Ridge Nature Reserve in Duluth, Minnesota is only one of them, and I have only been watching raptors there for two seasons, 2017 and 2018. Talk about "a very small fraction"!

There are many good poems, even great ones about birds of prey. A few of them are listed at the end of this book. As far as I know, however, this is the first and only illustrated collection of poems devoted solely to the raptor watching experience at one specific site. The poems are about raptors migrating south during the months of August through November at Hawk Ridge. It's about some of the people who work there, and it's about some of those who come from all over the country simply to witness the wonder of migration along the northern shore of Lake Superior.

Research scientists, field biologists, university professors, life listers, professional birding guides—they all study, know, and write about the science of raptors, but I've been wondering, even before I started on this book, whether there is anything to be known and written about the soul of birds. If we ask fifty ornithologists and fifty weekend bird watchers what they know or even what they think about the soul of birds, I'm sure we would get a hundred widely divergent, very intriguing responses. This book is my own attempt to ponder that question along with some thoughts about the soul of Hawk Ridge itself.

Hardly a day went by there, when I would be watching migrating raptors or listening to someone talk about them, that I did not uncover an idea for one or another of these poems. I take it for granted that this is precisely why there are so many birders in the world, young and old, who make the time, who take the time to watch, identify, attract, feed, study, ponder, research, call in, track, trap, band, capture, train, rescue, write about, think about, remember, imitate, seek, introduce others to, release, follow, glory in, fly with, stare at in open-mouthed amazement, capture on film, snap prize-winning photos of, paint, draw, protect, dissect, and connect with birds. There is never a dull moment during a birdwatching session. On the contrary, it fills us with an indefinable pleasure and even a sense of peace.

While writing this book, I did have a few notable experiences with raptors when I was not at Hawk Ridge. There are several poems in the collection about those experiences because they are reminiscent of something memorable that did occur at Hawk Ridge. For example, the first poem I wrote for this book, "Peregrine Over Hawk Ridge," led to my spending three months at home in the early spring of 2018 watching a family of Peregrine Falcons through a bird-cam installed in a nest box in St. Paul. The four poems in the Falco Peregrinus quartet on page 72 are about that family. The more time I spend at Hawk Ridge, the more I awaken to the world of raptors everywhere else.

Watching birds has been a family passion for as long as I can remember. Mom had always wanted to be a writer, and Dad took time off from his job at 3M to give watercolors a try for a while in his 30s, but with the raising of four sons taking up most of their time and resources, they had precious little time left over for these avocations. They knew their birds, however, and they always made time for bird watching with us. They taught us everything we knew about birds in those early years. We lucked into some additional tutelage living across the pond from Francis Lee Jaques and his wife Florence Page Jaques for whom birds were a way of life as well as two brilliant careers as nature artist and nature writer respectively. Many were the visits to the Jaques home to stand spellbound in their basement watching Lee's homemade and home-painted Iron Range mountain community and railroad or gaze in awe at all of the wildlife paintings in his studio. But while my three brothers pursued careers in science, my own path veered toward the humanities. I am delighted, therefore, to offer this book as evidence that all those childhood lessons, the visits to the Jaques home, the Audubon Christmas bird counts, visits with my brothers at work, the countless walks out the back door to fill the bird feeders and now regular visits to Hawk Ridge are not lost on me.

Hawk Ridge has given me an entry point back into my childhood, but more importantly, it has given me an entry point into, and a much deeper curiosity about the natural history of birds. The overflow of powerful feelings shows no signs of slowing down; I have come to understand why my family, my new friends at Hawk Ridge, and birders around the world are unswervingly passionate about birds, and especially so during migration. Raptor watching encourages us to imagine not only what the soul of a bird might be, but how that soul might have some connection to our own. Moreover, migration itself is a soulful and miraculous thing to witness. I hope that these poems and Penny's drawings will introduce you to or remind you of what the miracle of raptor migration is like not just at Hawk Ridge but around the world. Maybe they will even persuade you to head for one or another of the nationwide and the worldwide count sites to stand in awe at the miracle of hawks on high.

Phil Fitzpatrick
Duluth, Minnesota
January, 2019

In the Beginning . . .

Molly Evans and her husband David were two of the original members of Duluth's hawk watching community. Here, Molly recalls how it was years before Hawk Ridge had gained popularity. She and her fellow pioneers in hawk counting were committed, dedicated to a seriousness of purpose that is still practiced by the Hawk Ridge staff today.

oh, it was all so simple back then; for a while, we
just used tally marks on the back of an envelope,
whatever we could find; no crowds or computers

too chaotic now; the birds don't fly quite as low;
we were serious counters but didn't use clickers,
much too fancy; instead, we used the box method

Jack taught us that: four dots, four sides and an X
equals ten; he was the best, he always had some
little rhyme or song for the kids who were there

you know that Golden Eagle they caught once,
the one they rigged up to send signals back here?
well, they named that handsome bird after Jack

we used to lie back on that big rock and count;
folks would stop by n' ask what was going on;
back then, we only counted 'shins, broads n' reds

Jan, she was so good with details, she's the gal
got us thinking about our name; we used to be
Hawk Hill, but we changed it to Hawk Ridge

Jan mapped out the trails; she and John cut them;
we said no motorized vehicles n' the City agreed;
those trails are there yet today and still no motors!

Fud, that's Dave, doing that banding all alone
like clockwork for years without complaining,
dawn to dusk dutifully sending in his hawk data

was him first thought of using cans to carry 'em in,
those colored chip cans for sharp-shins, n' for reds
coffee cans; at last, we could show folks the hawks

no, it's not like it used to be: a handful of us then,
on an Indian Summer day lying on a rock counting
n' babbling along together under hawks and clouds

The Place and Its People

Perfect Duluth Day

it's one of those clear-as-a-bell days, the air feels clean
as if blown by warm mountain winds across a receding
glacier, the kind of air that makes you forget about the
receding glaciers in the world, all you want to do is stand
at the edge by the boulders and breathe deep as you gaze
out across the lake waiting for the broad-wings to arrive

Noel greets the newest visitors, an elderly Omaha couple
who have come to watch hawks every fall since they got
engaged up here forty-two years ago during senior year as
biology majors at UMD studying environmental education;
Julian attended John Green's geology classes while May, she
would volunteer with Jan doing hawk counts at Hawk Ridge

it's a great day for hawks, Noel sings out; they agree, and
as they walk past the trailer heading up to greet the counters,
they see a busy flock of exuberant cedar waxwings flying by
reminding them of the forty-two Septembers of waxwings
and days like this when it feels like the people and the birds
are all in the right place before the first hawks start to come

first broad-wings out over the golf course, shouts a counter
and even though May is still setting up tables while Julian
approaches new arrivals, they both lift up their binoculars
because, as they say, spotting the first hawks never gets old;
is this your first visit, Julian asks; the new visitors nod yes
so he takes them around to introduce them to the regulars

yes, this September day's a perfect one to break a record,
everyone agrees; the wind is from the northwest, and even
the clouds look perfect, educators going up the trail to teach
an early class of kids who have no idea yet what they're in for:
a box of surprises, a few cool games, and then a hawk release
into a sky as blue as it was the day Julian popped the question

Oracular Info

it takes some time
to learn the order
the proper order
in which raptors
riding ridge winds
will arrive and
everyone here who
already knows it
sounds like Tiresias
at Thebes or the Oracle
at Delphi telling you
broad-wings come first
sharpies too both long
before red-tails arrive
balds ride on through
from start to finish
but goldens you know
not until mid-October
Rough-legged Hawks
of course come last
and close the season
it doesn't take long
to learn the drill
especially if you listen
to the prophets
they're the ones
using the Swarovskis

Plumology

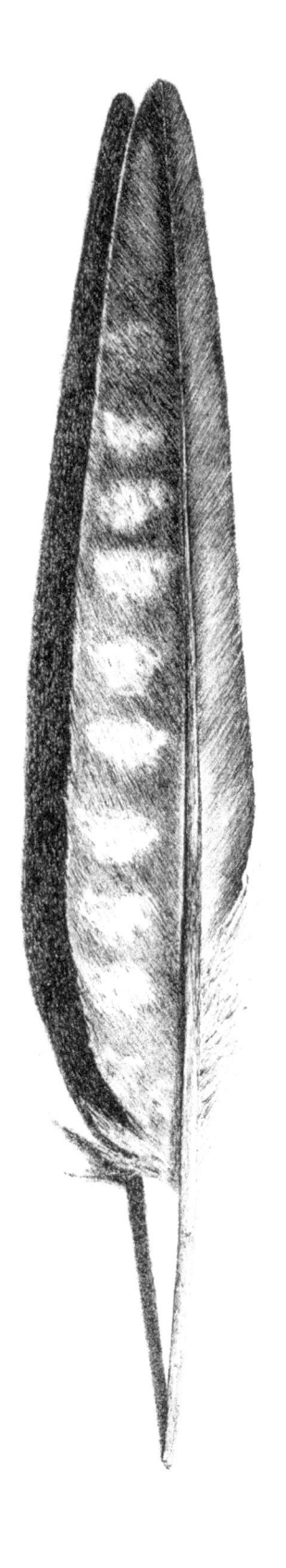

have you never stooped down to salvage
a time traveler resplendent in its solitude,
humble airy gift resting there at your feet,
its time on the wing, its service complete?

you've seen these emissaries at work, yes?
in pillows, dusters, and quill pens, these
exhibitionists showing off on fancy hats,
headdresses, and gaudy wraparound boas?

it is not given to us to know where, much
less when any feather's nubbined ancestral
filaments first appeared; no one was there,
feathers being that much older than history

ask exactly how, or perhaps try asking why
they first appeared for a better chance at an
untangled answer; but the questions keep
coming like broomsticks bringing water:

how many mya from scale to feather?
on what did the first feathers appear?
which reason for ungainly flight came first:
escape, food, display, warmth or safety?

was it a leap upward from earth's restraint,
or a more dramatic glide out and down
after an exploratory or hasty fearful climb?
was function first the chicken or the egg?

miraculous from whatever the lowly start,
an utterly arresting unspectacular design,
they are now complicated beyond measure
rainbow colors, myriad shapes and functions

learn big words and become a plumologist,
but why chase after that? go outside instead,
find a feather to hold, let that feather's color
tell you its ancient story, and when you do—

whether crow-black, finch-gold, bunting-blue,
seagull-white, cardinal-red or loon-flecked—
it will soar from Archaeopteryx across time
through your fingers and into your open soul

Lesson

(An imaginary conversation between interpreter and Hawk Ridge Count Director John Richardson and a Hawk Ridge newcomer. John is originally from England.)

Nice bald coming in underneath those clouds, now, folks.
    Whaddya mean, 'bald'? You mean a Bald Eagle?
Oh, sorry there, mate, yeah, that's a Bald Eagle, but we sometimes say "baldie" or "bald" for short.
    Okay. Well, just one question, then: Where's the white head?
He's only two or three. We call him a sub-adult.
    A what?
He's not an adult yet. He's a juvenile.
    Oh. You mean he's an eagle teenager, right?
Yeah, something like that, until he's five years old.
    What?
No white head and tail for five years.
    Then how do you know he's only *two*?
He's not dark enough to be any older.
    What?
Yeah, three and four-year olds, they get a bit darker.
    This guy looks pretty dark.
They get darker.
    Does it have to be that complicated?
Well, I don't make the rules. It is what it is, my friend. Oh, and then there's the eye color.
    Eye color?
Yep, It changes from brown to yellow.
    Huh!
See him now? Looks like he's headed for that kettle right out over the lake. See?
    See what? His eyes?
No, the kettle
    What?
That spiraling cluster of birds. Right beside all those wispy white clouds. See it?
    Yeah. What, I'm supposed to see their eyes from here?
NO! A kettle. *THAT'S* a kettle. All those birds. They're in what's called a kettle.
    Oh, okay . . .
Really? Okay?
    Yeah, okay, I see the, um, "kettle" . . . but, what about the eyes, now . . . ?
The eyes? Not much except that they change color over that five-year span. So does the beak.
    Naturally!
Anything else? You still on it?
    On it???
Do you still have that group of eagles in your view, in your binoculars.
    I guess you could say I'm "on it." Not having much luck seeing beaks and eyes.
No, they're too far away. But you can see the different plumages, can't you?
    Yeah, but they just look like black birds flying in a circle.

Well, that's what they are. You got *that* right.

    Hallelujah.

There's only one adult in that kettle, one that's at least five years old or older. Can you find it?

    You're kidding, right?

No. See if you can find it. It's the only one with a white head and a white tail.

    Dunno. No idea where to start. An' I'm getting tired. My neck's killin' me.

C'mon! Give it a try. He's toward the bottom. Move your glasses downward . . . *slowly!*

    Okay. I'm at the bottom. Where is he?

Good, good! Now, move your binoculars VERY slowly to the left. The adult is right there. See him?

    Not yet. They all look black to me.

Yeah, okay, let's wait a minute; maybe the sunlight will help us. You good for another minute or two?

    Yeah, yeah . . . but they look black to me, I'm looking at both edges . . .

They're all sub-adults except for that one at the edge. NOW! See him now? In the sunlight?

    . . . *OH, YEAH!!!* Now I see him. YEAH! The only adult, you say? Five years old, at least?

Yup! You got it, Pal.

    And the others are, what did you call them, "sub-something"?

Sub-adults. Juveniles. "Teenagers," I think is how you referred to them.

    Okay. I gotta quit. Like I say, my neck's killing me. And my arms are tired.

Okay. Good job. Well, done. Way to stay on that kettle.

    Can't wait to tell my wife. "Honey, I saw a kettle today, and I stayed on it!"

She'll be impressed.

    She'll be impressed, alright. Ha-ha-ha! She won't know what on earth I'm talking about.

Bring her up here tomorrow. The balds will still be here. It'll be a good day.

    Those same ones, the ones in that . . . what, *kettle?*

No, not them. They'll be long gone. New ones, I mean.

    Oh, okay. We'll see. That was kind of cool. Thanks for the lesson.

No problem, friend. No problem at all. You did well! Good job, mate!

    Sub-adult, kettle, juvenile . . . a whole new vocabulary

Yup. You'll be an expert in no time!

    Oh, I don't know about THAT. But thanks, anyway. See you tomorrow.

Good! Very good. So long.

Clinton

I cannot now recall ever meeting
a fellow who's every bit as genial
as he is congenial; he's a human
template, indeed, a living paragon
of both, one in whom neither trait
can obscure what the other offers

a true hawk whisperer showing us
the harrier's buff feathered wing
with all ten primaries fanned out
the bird's yellow eyes demanding
a timely finish to all this bother
soon, please, before a sure release

back from a sortie into the scrub
he appears to be empty-handed,
his thumb-and-forefinger clamp
judged but a casual affectation
until we spy the ghostly captive
he names autumn meadowhawk

assembling for his famous corvid class,
we traipse up the trail to a classroom
without walls, only a cloud-strewn
blue roof; it's neither bins nor bones
that wins us but gentle spoken spells,
the black magic of crow and raven

one busy Saturday, there was no cop
slowing cars, putting us on our guard
ambling dumbly across the dusty road;
for him, there is no Hawk Ridge job
any more important than another, so
out there he went to ensure our safety

look for him next time you're there;
learn migration patterns of the skies,
about the airborne biodiversity above,
distant origins, far-flung destinations;
attend to his gentle lessons gently told,
the interplay of words, wings and wind

Wizardry

not quite quick-change artists
these autumn trees and shrubs
their blithe metamorphosis
sneaks up surreptitiously
as you scan the sky watching
raptors kettle in the clouds

greens melt into yellows
in the lush lakeside carpet
while you snap the shutter
at hesitant hawks held up
Statue of Liberty-like in the
hands of breathless guests

on the hillside, the yellows
turn toward an orange thrill
two tardy red-tails cavort over
the reddening sumac clumps
among guard-rail boulders
and down the bashful slope

in October's too brief comfort
a dazzling pageant takes place
soaring red-tails pause to play
above the brilliant counterparts
floral wizards shifting visages in
dazzling sleight-of-leaf displays

Streaming

"Ah, but I may as well try and catch the wind."
– Donovan

uncountable feathered rapture, motes among the lazy clouds,
the distancing hawks command more than mere enumeration
and disappear from time to time into the infinite blue intensity;
languidly they circle, riding their reliable thermals ever upward

our imagination struggles with more than this improbability;
our intellect cannot piece together rising naked and unbuoyed
through the frigid height, boldly defying gravity far from the
security of nest or perch and losing definition to those below

upward they rise, and when some persuasive current arrives,
off they peel one or two at a time spooling straight south in line
numbered individuals for those to whom the job of counting falls,
to the rest of us, a far-off continuous ribbon of winged escape

Pringles Prize

The big ones do not fit; it's the little ones, the sharp-shins
that fit snug inside like a cigar in a tube, like a hand in a glove.
Perfect fit. Who first thought to adapt a Pringles can for this,

for this sweet little task? We know, of course, it was after '67—
no Pringles before that time. Colorful exterior, dark safety within.
They slip the banded hawk inside, a few a day when it is busy.

Here's a daily natural high: hawk in a bright horizontal tube, its tail
halfway out, carried up from the banding station; Allie disappears
behind the trailer, takes out the bird, a Cheshire Cat grin on her face.

The patient hawk, eased from its cardboard confines, squawks twice
before its obligatory role in the short show-and-tell begins, before it
lifts above wide-eyed kids who now love hawks even more than Pringles.

Legend

bumped into this guy up at Hawk Ridge once
at the edge of the dirt road, at early morning,
his forest-green Tundra, thread-bare duds
no fancy birding gear on or snappy logos
no broad gestures, big words, or phony talk
no bellowed hail-fellow-well-met greeting
pretty scruffy untamed air about him, just a
patchwork pine bark look, a Thoreau type
if y'know what I mean - I figured it was him;
everyone up there seems to know the guy,
I'd hear his name like rain drops on a pond:
Frank this, or Frank that, Frank Frank Frank
knows raptors from front to back, inside n' out;
word is a ton of banders started out with him
been at it as long as anyone here remembers,
another hawk whisperer type a' fella, they say,
say he's been to all the big raptor count sites
but doesn't wear any a' that stuff on his sleeve,
works more and talks less than most everyone;
knows Wisconsin good as he knows Minnesota;
if you get a chance to meet him, better take it
because around these parts, he's raptor royalty

The Uninvited Guest
~ 10/11/18 ~

remembering yesterday:

the uninvited guest overstays the welcome
    it has not been offered
with all of its calling cards on full display
    it muscles its way in
has its way with us, drives us back into our cars
into our Patagonias, North Faces and Eddie Bauers
locked inside snaps, straps, and zippers

but nine-hundred sixty seven sharpies do not care
their flaps are equal to the task
their low-flying urgency
    ducking under the golden hardwoods
jumping on rogue tailwinds
    making up for lost time
        making a go of it
            making us work hard
with our binoculars buried
our gloved hands clutching travel mugs close
    no
they do not care about any of it
but the push of it, flap and go

the juvenile red-tail does not care either:
    ride the wild winds back and forth
    spread your creamy wings
    catch every gust
    barely any need
    for even one flap
the utter necessity of it all
to work this midday wind for all it is worth
to stretch the proud pinions to their limit
to spread the ruddy tail feathers
    below us, above us and finally
        leaving us behind
            held hostage
by the cold relentless uninvited guest

You Can Have It Both Ways

you look up into the gray sky
       nothing
why is there anyone here, you wonder
lines of cars and a mix of enthusiasts
all of them bundled up
       the steady arrivals
            something is here,
            an energy or just
            a strong will to stay
            for now, a mystery
for all the commotion, there should be kettles
       scads of binoculars upraised,
           hubbub, scurrying about,
and chatter that is perky, endless, relevant,

then the eagle, the ravens, and there
       too close for comfort
            a little hawk shoots through,
its belly, the streaks, and the long tail:
you could reach up and almost grab it,
you duck in time to miss nearly being hit
by an adult Turkey Vulture his pink head
scanning the roadside as he glides past;
the sunlight breaks through bouncing
off the gleaming black feathers overhead

for there being really nothing in the sky,
and just as the counter announces a lanky
Northern Harrier's lackadaisical passage,
you wonder why so many birds fly so low,
and word comes from an expert walking by
(as if you should have already known it) that
they fly low when the wind is from the south
       oh, you say to yourself:
            of course
and raise your binoculars to count
all the rust-colored tail feathers
on the lone Red-tailed Hawk easing past
above your newly wise, oh-so-omniscient head

Redtail Release

gently his hands clamp on the Red-tailed Hawk
he looks like he is holding a ticking time bomb
bending over, he lowers it almost to the ground
the bird has no idea it will soon regain its wings
which are its life, no choice now but to be patient
listening to the count, the man prepares to let go
he will likely release more than just a wild bird

as one, hands and hawk gather speed skyward, but
at the point of release, I imagine an extra second
when his outstretched fingers pause a futile instant
wishing to have one more precious contact moment,
but the wingbeats are already way ahead of all that
carrying the tawny bird back into the morning air
beyond the reach of men and up over the rooftops

as if the hawk's feathers relished every slight breath
in the new heights, they tip in and out, they curl up,
wings and tail tilt effortlessly lifting the hawk higher
in a gentle looping excursion above yellow aspens
the brisk wind carrying it back and forth playfully
perhaps it is going through the process of forgetting
a strange new memory, regaining a deeper older one

Kaitlyn's Wow

from the first, her beatific smile:
it's a mile wide and taking on
the gusty day single-handedly;
it's windier than all get out now,
and while it is not snowing yet,
you see scads of scarves and hats,
heavy gloves, and puffy jackets
all crushing in right in front of her,
a bonfire of color in harsh wind chill
making it hard to find a good spot
among these Michelin Man outfits;

look: has she no gloves to wear?
her fingers are bare; give her a pair!
my Heavens, she must be freezing;
we sure are, and we lean inward
to learn, to listen, transfixed by her
sleight of hand moves, use of props
bird silhouettes, finger-sized objects
like talons and feathers, real wings
of owls, hawks, and ospreys all while
her solar heater of a smile warms
and delights us and banishes the cold;

a plastic tub at rest on the table
lurches in a sudden gust and becomes
an instant joke: oh, she shrieks without
skipping a beat, it seems that my tub
has plans to migrate, too! we laugh
as her warmth and wit merge, as if
we have come not just to meet, but to
huddle and watch, embrace her magic,
her tub of tricks each trick offered with
a snappy brazen joyful legerdemain;
we are reluctant to depart since heat
today comes as hard-earned as progress
does for the raptors we are here to see
whose scarcity in an unseasonable wind
Kaitlyn's wow makes very easy to ignore

Tarsometatarsus
a closer look at the leg of a Sharp-shinned Hawk

she's small, stealthy, and wicked fast
   a woodland rocket streamlined
      built to maneuver, built for speed
         look at that scaly pencil-thin bone
            that faded yellow spindle of a leg
               adapted to turn forests into kill zones

that bone is no femur, and, no, it's not a fibula
   it can't be a shin bone much less the tibia,
      a leg bone, yes partly, but partly is far from exactly
         it's a fusion-bone, you might say, a kind of bone-blend
            a hybrid, an aberration uniquely avian, but so much more

some ankle mixed with a bit of foot
   not more advanced, really, nor less but
      affording different permissions:
         to scratch the soil for seed
            to walk on lily pads
               to climb tree trunks
                  to snag fish out of the water
                     or to paddle on it, certainly
                        to wade through it with stealth

that bone is a departure for birds, alright, but hers is unlike
   that of any other raptor for her departure departs
      driven by a rare and singularly unusual skill:
         to snare songbirds on the wing
            snatch them right out of midair
               take a look at that leg bone once more
                  with that raised keel-shaped ridge
                     now look at it again, the whole of it

take a good look, it's one of a kind
   laterally compressed, bony, exquisitely long
      shaped over time into its pale-yellow length
         descended from a few mostly flightless
            but winged and scaly ancestors named
               Archaeopteryx, Aurornis Xui, or Yi qi;
            nothing more and nothing less
               than a single spectacular signature feature
                  developed through epochs of refinements
                     a steady stream of late Jurassic experiments

High-Interest Loan

grasping the dark Rough-legged Hawk
with two hands, one on top of the other
begins a short-term high-interest loan
with interest compounding by the minute
accumulating in a mostly invisible way;
standing on the top step while the dozen
bundled spectators crane for a clear look
or click an infinity of pictures or get closer
just to reap a tangible long-term benefit
from the proximity of the captive free-bird
whose majestic pinioned wings silently lend
their keeper's reverent hands just enough
of their mystic capital thereby affording him
a momentary grasp of a luxurious dividend.

spellbound by what I am holding up
my hands not quite clamping just pinning
both its eponymously shaggy yellow legs,
I move it gently from side to side both of us
staring mutely, statue-like straight ahead
a magnificent stillness of its rounded head
a primal well-designed perfect little asset
my instructions seem so short, so simple
in my mind, I long to be given twice as many
that I might release time in the bird's place,
that I could make bold our escape, roughie
and I, to a spot not far away where I could
twist my hands just enough to see his eyes,
where I could— "On three, one two three!"

opening suddenly, unbidden by this dreamy
head of mine, my hands in concert swing up,
burst apart freeing the hawk back to its own,
its known, its welcome necessary airy world
a composition of mere air, sky, clouds, trees,
and migration's annual and irresistible pull;
the banding done, the unwilling emissary waits
its short indenture more of gift than a loan,
a mid-flight concession, quick trade of which
we, an awed curious somewhat wistful band
of wingless walkers, cannot get nearly enough
and to whom this morning chill blowing in
on a numbing northeast wind means nothing
but more, means all: a windblown chance at
borrowing from the sky another winged envoy

Everybody's an Expert

easy to be at ease up here,
     but easy not to be, too;
easier, perhaps, to be up there
     at ease
     an airborne silhouette
     a soaring speck
like that one
     over the water tower
or that one
     above the school
     crossing under that puffy rabbit-cloud
or the one circling over the platform
     straight up from the sign
     right of the van, beside the tall pine
look for the wings on a dihedral
the elongated fingers, the pale head, and tippy,
the scattered voices yell;
first you have to find it, someone whispers;
use your naked eye, then the binos
someone else says, so what is it?
     Turkey Vulture, says a voice
     there's another one now, see?
Hey, sharp-shin coming over
     watch the flap-flap-glide
(naked eye naked eye naked eye)
and the long straight tail; now, see whether
     it's squared off or not
         short stubby wings
(now the binos, the binos: hurry!)
so what is it, a sharpie? Yes, a sharp-shin
can't see any shins, sharp or dull; whaddya mean?
you'll see if they bring one up from the banding station
there's only one up there; where are the rest?
it's a south wind; you have to read the wind
     hatch-year male, and remember:
the males are smaller than the females . . .
     need to find a new group now,
must be time to change locations
     listen harder
         look longer
             ask questions
they all know so much, there is
     so much to be known,
         and everybody's an expert

Of Time, Space and History

Hawks on High
– for Yvonne

a friend I know
says she went up there once
went up to Hawk Ridge
says she expected to see
streams of hawks on high
tells me everyone always says
that's what you see
on any autumn Hawk Ridge day
you see streams of hawks on high

but, she says, I only saw three;
where were they, those streams
the streams of hawks on high,
she asks looking bereft
as though she had lost a thing,
lost a gift or a treasure;
where were they, those streams,
the streaming hawks on high?

those streams will come, I say,
yes, I assure her, go back there;
return to Hawk Ridge some day
some orange and blue autumn day
when the wind is fresh in your face
as you look toward the north,
and they will come in scores,
hundreds even, some days thousands
they will fly both low and high
under the brilliant Hawk Ridge sky
among white clouds on autumn winds
they will be there, they will come
migrating, circling, soaring streams
the wondrous and streaming
miracle of hawks on high

That Old Gang of Mine

I could name you a half-a-dozen or so,
but that would be a distraction; there is
no disrespect meant, take it from me:
they come, and they've been coming,
in fact, for decades, can you imagine that?

couples come like migrants themselves
to check on the day's counts, to learn
whether they can help gain a few converts,
all the remember-when stuff, the stories,
receiving the unspoken homage that is so
richly deserved from young and old alike,
though those are surely not as old as they

impassioned zealots of the annual count
can't resist the annual urge to climb the steps
and hob nob with The Chosen Ones, young
though they might be that day, with their
binos up or leaning over a scope, counting
and chattering like a colony of capuchins

no matter what day or what time it is
their smiles are true, they know things,
and there is nothing they have not seen;
I saw one at breakfast today who saw me
and said hello; next week, I'll dine with two
of Hawk Ridge's legends who've seen it all;
you know, someone should write a book

But Who's Counting?

on Wednesday, August 16th, 2017
at the Hawk Ridge Nature Reserve platform
Karl counted *one* blue darter
there were *none* for two more days
then *five* on Saturday, *six* more on Sunday,
five Monday, *six* Tuesday . . .
by month's end,
more than *thirty* a day flew over,
and on Sunday, September 24,
they counted *two thousand five hundred fifteen;*
during the ten o'clock hour alone
five hundred sixty-four by Alex's count;
on Sunday, November 12th a little after noon,
Stephen saw one more,
the *twenty-two thousand one hundred sixty third* one,
the final Sharp-shinned Hawk of the season;
that's just *four hundred thirty-nine* fewer
than were counted the previous year
during the same period of time;
2016 was the peak year - that's
a lotta sharpies over those two seasons

but hold on:

compare that total
to the *sixty-two thousand one hundred twenty-three*
Broad-winged Hawks
the counters at Hawk Ridge tallied
during the same two-year period

    and

look what happened in 2003:
on Monday, September 15,
they counted *one hundred one thousand six hundred ninety-eight* of them;
why, from three to four in the afternoon alone,
they counted
thirty-one thousand twenty-four;

that's just in *one* hour
and only *one* species

but wait, there's more
now that we're talking broad-wings:

during that same two-year period,
in Corpus Christi, Texas
at Hazel Bazemore County Park,
counters logged a total of
*seven hundred fifty-five thousand
one hundred twenty-six!*

    and then, then . . .

        then there's Veracruz . . .

Extinction Event

and how will the next one look
the one going on now
the one that looks
unspectacular
until it becomes spectacular
until the floods and the fires
determine how it will look
for the foreseeable future?

I can hear the footsteps, can't you?
I see the feathers on the ground
they are scattered on the ground
they are buried in the ground
they are not in the air
the feathers are not in the air
anymore

Rhetorical Question

lulled into this half-sleep
watching a few minutes
of a low Red-tailed Hawk's
luxurious fall afternoon's
ridgetop drift and wondering
if, aided by some elaborate
and finely ground eyepiece
or, perhaps, a device built
to slow wingbeats down to a
more visible per second rate,
this bird's feathered flight was
deconstructed to the point
it was a series of minute twitches,
could I, could anyone be alert
enough to see a solitary beat,
and deem it in any way at all
superfluous?

In the early part of the Twentieth Century, men went out to sites along migratory flyways and shot raptors out of the sky just for sport. The carnage was devastating. Eventually, outraged citizens who had long been gathering up wounded birds for rehabilitation and humanely disposing of the dead ones took action to halt this slaughter once and for all. Hawk Mountain Sanctuary in Kempton, Pennsylvania was one such site, and so was Hawk Ridge. Thanks to a handful of conservation-minded pioneers, hundreds of sanctuaries and counting sites like Hawk Ridge now exist across North America.

Dead Hawks

in those crisp long-ago shotgun months of autumn
gatherers would carry from the forests, baskets full
of flightless dead hawks, broad-winged, red-tailed
and more, most with a spattered blood-red dressing,
torn or broken wings and mangled feathers all askew
vacant crinkled eyes robbed of any last chance to see
their soaring companions in the welcoming horizon;
some were under bushes to where they had flopped
cringing wounded and fearful of another harsh report,
some caught mid-plummet dangling by broken tails
or talons and hanging helpless, their fall interrupted
by some crook in a dark net of indifferent branches;
on occasion, furtive tears fell on a singular tawny belly
or a drooping head wetting the crusted blood making
it a brighter red even as the tentative gloved fingers
soothed a rumpled feather or arranged a lifeless wing
as if these birds with limp-necked bodies had been,
by some kind miracle, still taking breath in their glory
and were only a few beats, heart and wing, from dignity

Surmising

what's been eating at me lately is
how long a million years really is
    one
        million
            years
that's a one followed by   ready?
six zeros   yes
    that many years
wouldn't just *two* zeros be enough, or
five times a Bald Eagle's life expectancy?
but *six* . . .
you and I and all the other hominids
back to mister and mrs h. erectus themselves
have been on *our* little walk across
this planet, leaving more than our share
of collateral damage behind,
in *very* round numbers fewer than,
    just shy of, not quite, but almost
two
    million years
yes, think of *that*:
    but *that's*
        a paltry smidgen
of the number of zeros I strain to grok,
strain like Sisyphus rolling his unruly rock
up the eternal hill, and that is, how many mya
since some bony membraned intrepid pterosaur
vaulted its colossal webbed clumsiness
what could not have been any more than
a few miraculous feet into the primeval air
word has it, though,
    or it appears that,
        or so we are told that evidence suggests,
even *proves* that *that* staggering experiment
morphed into a dead end, a losing proposition,
doomed to fail, an evolutionary cul de sac
a few hundred mya down the line
as far as staying aloft went, as far as
winning command of the ancient skies went, and
that the *real* fliers, their therapod cousins, in fact,
were the very ones whose sleek descendants
now, today, work their September soar,
their wondrous way down along Hawk Ridge

Hawk Eye

why the space instead of just hawkeye
with that little Mohican resonance?
maybe a Mash or Marvel one as well;
only one word in Iowa, no question:
"Capitalize it" proud locals admonish

what is certain, though, is the thing,
the very thing itself, the hawk's eye;
barely takes a second, less than one,
to know, to succumb to the spell of
two black discs inside colored irises

they hold and lock you, no apology
no thought possible in the hypnosis
not of age gender species or history
nothing—the fastening disarms you
wonder fixed in an unblinking stare

ignore the miracle the eyes contain
holding secrets eons old in the cold
pierce of their gaze, with much to say
of plain survival, fighting odds thrown
before them by time, nature, and man

as etched on walls of caves or tombs
we have enlisted their hunting talents
there is a time-defying mythic bond
a linkage not asking or yielding more
than a conditional very reluctant deal

little of the wild is left in canine eyes:
its spell was long ago duly tamed out,
but migration's tug all but guarantees
the fierce wildness in a raptor's eyes;
the hunt is all, death their only defeat

what to draw from this cold sharp fix
evolved to the degree that it must hide
much more than hawk eyes ever reveal;
but, why expect more than we can earn
from tools adept at hiding what's within?

39

Kettle

a hawk is a hawk is a hawk
might be one glib way to think of
this eyeful, a sky full of them

a single Broad-winged Hawk aloft
can't be any different from the rest
in these majestic autumn spirals

one gyre, its hundreds of hawks
circling, a reverse whirlpool at once
unique and identical to gyres past

September curiosity asks questions
of the complex ageless phenomenon
with its signature annual message

can we track countless generations
back to some era, epoch, or period
when raptors first rode updrafts here?

migration's absolute necessity is really
more a matter of how than it is of when
easier to mull than mute bony numbers

what force or habit, or maybe Hand
was at work in what dim age ago
to give raptors their climb and soar?

how unspeakably wise to know when
to flap, to bank, and when to stream
leaving us craning and anchored below

Ghost Birds

it happens this way sometimes on a field
over a meadow or above the breathy lake
away from daily hubbub at Hawk Ridge:
while the dog lopes leash-free, a quiet sit
knowing hawks are elsewhere but not here,
no need to bother with hope or expectation

yet long I stare skyward for empty minutes
at gray clouds scudding under white puffs,
a classic midday sky with intermittent blue;
then, an apparition: a dozen distant specks,
a spiraling gyre of broad-wings, ghost birds;
don't look away, they will not remain long

the wonder is how on earth, how in heaven
the winged transients could have come here,
could have taken shape, stayed long enough
for threads, for traces of older ghosts to visit;
how they found this moment stays shrouded,
but memories renew as they fade from view

Whiteness, for Instance

it's the time thing again
trying to grasp what its
passing is all about
it cannot be merely about
the rapid flow of this minute
from yesterday, from last year
ever backward into oblivion -
or can it?

to begin with, consider
how much time it has taken
for the Bald Eagle's shimmering
hood to become white: it didn't
just happen overnight, did it?
think of that odd appearance,
of a couple of not-brown feathers
ages before Tenochtitlan
or Stonehenge or the Pleistocene

persistent white a myriad of epochs
gone by; civilizations have come
and they have gone, the eagles
have seen them all bearing
the white of their feathers as
unaware of that history as now
I am awakening to and gaining
only the merest of inklings,
but today, when I see the scores
maybe the hundreds of Bald Eagles
soaring south from breeding grounds,
that whiteness and the work of ages
it carries does not pass overhead
very lightly at all

Headset Hawk

unfold the two miracles on your back
their feathers have been telescoped
in and out an infinite number of times
in all the years of your wild amazing life
power them up, pull back down again
lift skyward joining others on the move

feel the elemental zephyrs do their best
to make you a plaything; but you know
what to do: your tail works a turn, a lift
as your wings redirect the wily wind and
effortlessly make, from this rival, an ally
with the merest of delicate adjustments

the ground and its inhabitants diminish
the landscape is opening below you now
limitless sources of safety, food and rest;
scan the distance for familiar landmarks
how simple to glide with so little sacrifice
to ride the wind again to your safe harbor

The How of It

it's got to be something more
than that internal clock thing;
if it's merely genetic material,
it might as well be string theory,
moral compass, or ham on rye

these birds fly unmotivated by
an alarm clock, a calendar, or
a straw boss with a clipboard;
no whistling cowpoke drives
this feathered stampede south

and consider the multiples we
are talking about here: billions;
not the mind-numbing number
of millennia it has taken them
to come this far along in time,

nor is this about populations
though that might be fitting,
no small order of magnitude
there; but no, it is only about
codes or modes of risk/reward

a book's coming out over here,
a leading authority says there:
no, the conclusive experiments,
endless tests, methods of inquiry
fail to measure, or to measure up

the mystery remains a mystery
about which science only says
we don't quite know for sure, or
what we do know is only this,
or, as far as can be determined . . .

channel Frost: something there is
that does not love an answer;
we know they fly from here to there,
that it's about scarcity and survival:
it's the how of it we can't yet answer

First Migrant

unimaginably barren
neither a wild outback
nor a wasteland or void
nothing like the bush, just
a trackless inhospitableness
no cultivation or order
an unchecked Mesozoic tangle

now dream up or picture somewhere
in the barren Cretaceous scorch
    an ungainly hulking toothless
        string of hybrid beasts
straining right through
    their young scaly
        restless earthbound lives
to shed fur, to elongate toes
    to shorten and flare tails
a Jekyll-and-Hyde interminable squirm
over a yawning epochal eternity
    trying against all the laws
of nature
    of physics
        of gravity
            of history
to rise up
    escape
        and win

Black on Gray, October 29
– remembering Dad

The absence of color is hardly an excuse. That corvid
    is certainly not afraid to call attention to itself.
It appeared out of the limitless gray
    while the blue was on lunch break.

I cannot see exactly what it is,
    but it looks like he is dragging something.
The kids in that class do not notice a thing;
    it appears that no one is going home.

The day is lousy with crows. When I listen closely,
    I can always picture him at breakfast
        whistling like a meadowlark.

Dramatis Personae

Peregrine Over Hawk Ridge

trackless tracer
record holder
soundless
black bullet-bird
cloud piercer

up-tilted binoculars
whip around
the hurried yells
where, *WHERE!?*
there, and then
not

the pale blue
empty canvas
all that remains
but the ghost of that
dark blur yet
plummets through
at least one
stunned memory

Black Quintet

two in front, three behind
wing-shaped formation,
a squadron of stealth fighters
fast smooth deft and quiet
scarcely any flap
flying straight above
right to left, north to south

what stories do these ravens
harbor in their wings
in their bright black bodies
in their sleek souls?

winter winds whispering
through lofty pines,
lichen-covered granite cliffs
plunging into ancient lakes,
drenching rains beneath
primeval pyrotechnics,
the ear-splitting crack
of summer storms,
timeless boreal rhythms
enveloping only occasional
insignificant two-leggeds

what a collective memory
this black quintet must carry
in their transient corvid souls
on their purposeful journey
over the borderless landscape
to the ancient winter place

Little Blue Darter, or the Aha Moment

what'd you call it? a little blue darter? what's a blue darter?
ah, it's a bird hawk, you know, used to be called a bullet hawk,
   a sparrow hawk, or maybe a chicken hawk, but it's a sharp-shin,
      a sharpie, Sharp-shinned Hawk, smallest of the American accipiters
         acceptors? . . . um, acceptors of what?
No: accipiter . . . ack-SIP-it-ter!
         oh . . . wait, but didn't you say blue darter at first?
Yeah, but that's just an expression: blue for the slate-gray cape
   around the head and shoulders of the adult birds
      like a solitary soldier from the Confederacy
         and darter for faster-than-the-eye-can-see
            woodland maneuverability
               predatory sorties in the forest and
                   feathers-everywhere surprise attacks
                      bald-faced midair songbird kills
   okay, so is this one here a blue darter?
no, no, that one's a Cooper's Hawk . . . same genus but . . .
      genius? now I'm really confused!
No, genus, JEE-nis . . .okay, okay, never mind; that's just science-speak
   they're similar, related but different; a sharpie has a small rounded head
      and a long squared-off tail, not rounded like that one, see?
         so, we put this one next to that one, and . . . see what I mean?
      okay, yeah, I see . . . but why sharp-shinned, then?
very good question, and not many field guides answer it either, so, ready?
         sure . . . I'm in this far; you might as well take me all the way!
good; okay, this . . . this is the other big difference; look . . . see
      what, that leg?
yep, that's the one; what do you see?
      looks like any other bird leg: long and skinny and yellow
look at it again, more closely this time . . .
      m-m-m-m . . .
and think about the name while you're looking at it . . .
      blue darter?
NO! . . . the other name!
      oh . . . okay, you mean, what was it, um . . . sharp-skinned hawk?
Ah . . . no, *that* would be impossible, sharp skin, ha-ha! Sharp-shinned Hawk. *Shin.*
      Okay, okay, Sharp-shinned Hawk, but I still don't . . . Ohhhh, a-HA!
      Sharp shins. Now, I get it! Pretty sharp, eh?
Very sharp. Aha, indeed.

Parallax

is that you, again, old man
watching and wondering
down there on the lonely overlook?
go ahead and wonder on
flight is my birthright
you have yours, I have mine
there are no questions
that can or should be asked
it is all about time,
time and readiness
I know the sense of your thoughts;
like arrows they pierce the sky
around me as I fly

yes I am lucky, but
the luck is hard won
it lasts a mere moment
you, too, are lucky
rooted down there on the diabase
disappearing behind me
as the orange sunset fades ahead
you have your moment, too
find your own wings, old man;
wonder if you must,
but live now, this season
live the next as well
soon enough, we will both
return to earth

Harrier Brown

brown there is beyond a doubt
of the humble unassuming type
but now consider harrier brown
a brown to which other browns
are quite obliged to bow down
for upon deeper scrutiny, on more
exacting inspection, there appears
a brown of a mesmerizing sort here,
a confident and radiant brown
that emanates from breeze-blown
breast feathers in quiet gossamer
profusion, an ordered overlapping,
a cinnamon pillow layered gently,
underlain by a creamy buff sheath
a quiet subtle buoyant under-down;
toward the crown is yet another
deeper hearty robust kind of brown
clearly broken into dramatic thirds:
collar, eye ring, and a mottled pate
not-quite of a dark chocolate hue,
more the look of homemade fudge
though no taste here will be essayed
guarded by the fiercest wild eyes
the unblinking yellow-black orbs
discs above an unforgiving frown,
and the clamped unyielding beak
would just as soon duly dispatch
even the most innocent of fingers,
the most inquisitive of onlookers,
to protect its proud harrier brown

Double Gos Tease

all around the country, and I do mean *all* around it,
there are sites like ours, but now, it is all right here,
it is right now, at Hawk Ridge, this day as we watch
two adult Northern Goshawks soaring at what seems
like fifty miles high or more, twisting tilting turning

they look connected like two synchronized swimmers:
when one banks left, the other banks, too, in strict unison;
the binos grow heavier, but I dare not lower them, for
these dark-winged dancers will become less than specks,
so I watch on; it is more than what it seems, I tell my arms

what is it about these two? I've seen twinned hawks before;
they tumble and right themselves like acrobats performing
no idea how impossibly high, I cannot even hazard a guess;
they linger, climb, circle, rarely a flap, still plainly attached,
I feel the connection keenly; the binos have lost their weight

why, they are teasing me, I think; yes, teasing me in tandem
this miraculous duet is in my mind but is no less a miracle;
is thinking possible under a thought-defying high-wire act?
lowering my arms, I look around to find the rest have left;
the hawks, too, drift away; I alone own the distant dance

Tee Vee

oh, soaring buzzard in black
you and your sunlit pals
with those skinny pointed
finger-feathers at the tips of
your always wide wings in a vee
and skinheads like thugs
so unsightly, small and naked
what rotting heap of carrion
do your scavenger's eyes espy?
but never mind the questions

for the dreamy jet-black sheen
of your quiet feathers hushes us
your signature wobbly dihedral
catches the noonday brilliance
in your indolent hypnotic gyre
out over Superior's shimmer;
ignore our usual *what died?* trope
born of witnessing a few too many
TV westerns, ample roadkill, and
decades of your eternal circling

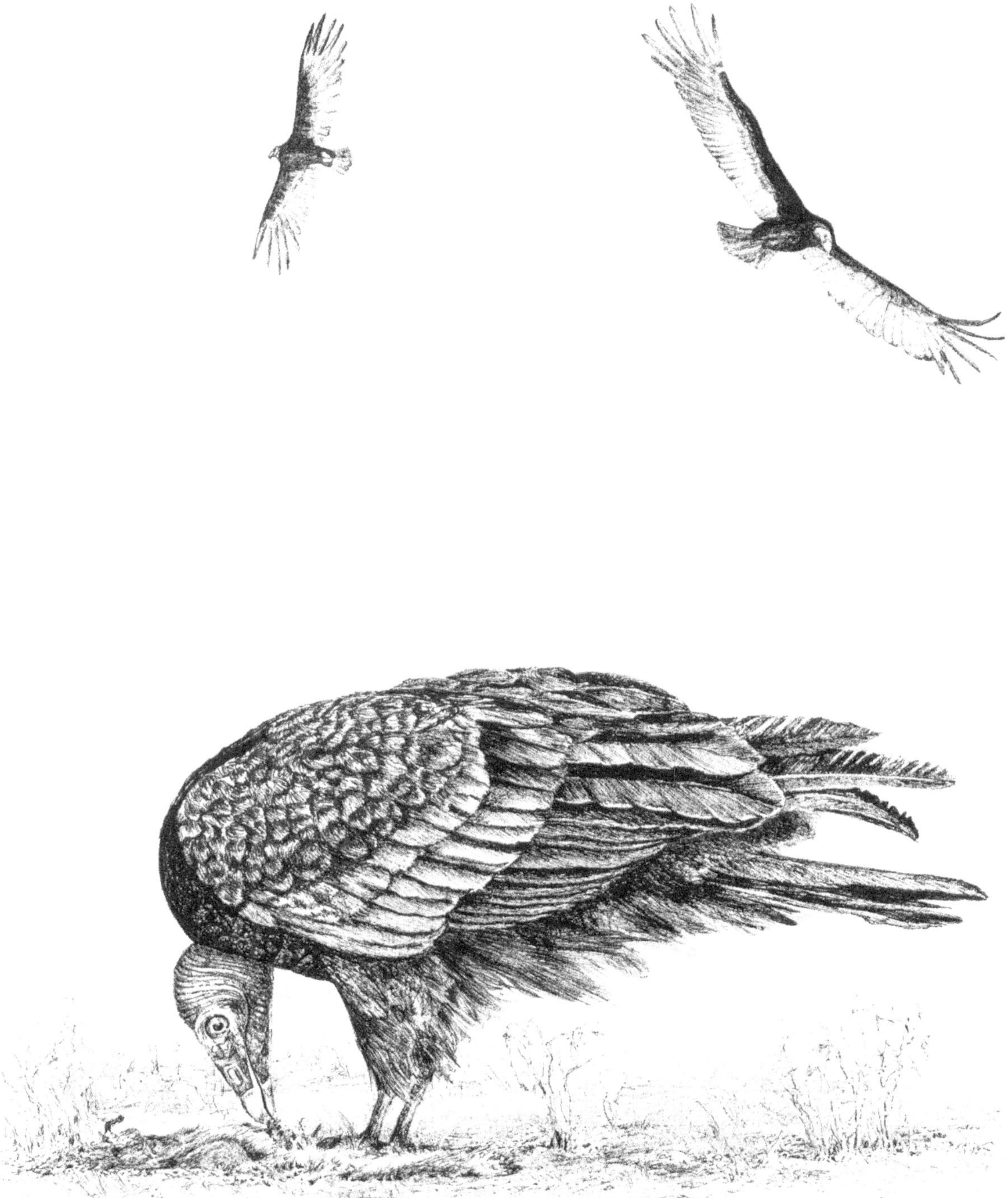

Better Late Than Later

these late-autumn robins are one thing:
loosely organized treetop bands, fluffy
pompous and foraging in the dead leaves
like mendicant friars with a bit of derring-do
that flies in the face of this early fall chill,

but a sextet of effervescent Eastern Bluebirds
in peppy undulating flight like goldfinches
and flying low over the observation platform
boasting their own thrushy brand of courage?
now, that's a bird of an entirely different color!

moments before the sound of their perky warble
(a more familiar song on the nearby golf course)
comes the loud call from a hawk-deprived counter
announcing these six in their mellifluous flyover
bouncing along as if it was more May than October

I blurt out the words *"better late than later!"* but it
seems a flimsy retort given the better-than-even odds
they have their wingy reasons for hanging around 'til now;
they are late, but I hear them say, now well on their way,
"look to your own preparations, friend; winter's coming!"

The Big One

"Looking into an eagle's eye changes you."
– Charles Post, in his film Sky Migrations

they all know I will be looking out for it today
like a crazed Ahab looking out for The White Whale
I am on the lookout for The Big One, the golden one;
my crow's nest is this bluff overlooking Superior
my spy glass the binoculars raised to my eyes
I am searching the clear blue expanse above;
like Ishmael on the mast-head, I fear the dizziness
from the sky's sheer and uninterrupted infinity;
the ocean below him is the blue vault above me
be careful say the staff; *that sun will scorch your eyes!*
kettles of soaring Red-tailed Hawks distract me
lull me with lazy loops so impossibly high up
and I have not seen The Big One yet, the one
with the golden nape I know I will never truly see
always up there somewhere adrift in the blue sky
as The White Whale still swims the blue deeps

the sudden cry sounds interrupting my azure spell:
Golden Eagle! Left of the sun in the cloud over the flag!
and for a blue moment, I hear a faint *Thar she blows!*
solitary and black, the bird swims into my dazed view;
unmindful it is the object of an insignificant searcher,
it soars miles above where my Melvillian imagination,
or any puny piece of equipment, any artist's ambition
might reach; in my binocular view, it is only a speck,
a slow-motion glider in the morning flow of migrants;
I try in vain to memorize this dark dreamy glimpse
composed less of details than an ancient wistfulness,
and as the sun drives me away and apart from what
my eyes, in a kind of resigned squint, and my mind
in that desperate human way, try gamely to retain
(and what now is scarcely more than a dim vision),
I hold fast to my certainty of the bird's quintessence

Ingrid, the Lapland Longspur

she is not from Lapland, assuredly,
perhaps once, she they name Ingrid;
better to be too busy than be lonely
hopping between roadside boulders
drawn by scattered cracker crumbs
and seeds, the last few autumn bugs

she's alone, here three days they say,
an outlier from the customary flock
of frenetic migrant longspurs, she's
in no particular hurry to depart given
no extreme southern destination nor
any urgent survival alert, like snow

bit of an exhibitionist is this Ingrid,
unafraid of gawkers, the kind with
garish bazooka-style camera lenses;
unfazed by occasional canines, and
quite content is she, looking more
sparrowish in her banal winter garb

her solitude becomes her these gray
shoulder-season days and prompts
questions of a deeper sort regarding
her readiness for winter, the strength
to go it alone, settling now for seeds,
insects being in sudden short supply

Miracle Missed

*For of all sad words of tongue or pen,
the saddest are these: "it might have been."*
   – John Greenleaf Whittier

A leucistic red-tail, the newspaper says.
Hardly an everyday miracle, but I missed it.
The newsprint tells the story; the headline
Could just as easily read, "You fool! Idiot!
You missed it. Where on earth were you?"

Miracles can yet be miracles if no one
Is there to witness them. If the hawk
Had flown past, gone a different way,
Chosen a different day, who's to say
It wouldn't have been, still be a miracle?

Might knowing a thing exists be enough
In bird watching and in other things, too?
Might our five senses be quite unnecessary
When it comes to these everyday miracles?
Alone, this miracle itself might be enough.

Consider the satisfaction of just knowing
A miracle existed once or even exists today:
Dinosaurs, a rose's red, a snow-white hawk.
What delight there is in the mere reckoning
Of luck, of time in shaping these wonders.

One Hundred Fifty Mya

comes the ancient question again, always,
in labs, museums, classrooms, in the field,
as to isolating exactly when birds first flew
never mind migration's elusive born-on date

it's nothing but a shell game most of the time,
this job of pinpointing a date that possesses
ample accuracy and a foolproof fossil record
to give it prominence in a three-stanza poem

best to exchange stares with that banded raptor
until its steely resolve unlocks your imagination
hushing the talk; now, envision the initial trial,
the monumental first successful liftoff or leap

Jack

Golden Eagle in a binocular view
the epitome of oxymoron because
you cannot magnify magnificence
it's better calmly to lower the binos
and watch this cynosure of a raptor
only with the eyes, its wing feathers
savoring the zephyrs in stately soar
nobility adrift in an infinity of blue;
try not to picture a shaggy gold nape
its keen, alert, sculpted countenance
the yellow pierce of its cere and eye
sharp hook of its pointed black beak
the windblown look of a cloud god;
better, instead, to inquire about Jack
banded respectfully here six years ago
fitted with a feather-light transmitter
released forthwith to teach as he flies
he's pictured cradled in Frank's arms;
follow his immense migration loop,
the purple map line reveals very little,
barely anything past a heroic distance
2,000 hard miles from spring breeding
above harsh Northwest Territory waters
to the Missouri Ozark winter terminus

Jack, Jack, would that the eagle
on this November morn was you;
no stopover today, nothing doing!
you'd have miles to go, Jack, miles;
Jack on the wing, daring no stop,
leave the rest behind, leave them
at their easy winter river retreat;
you gave us your best once, Jack,
and once was enough; fly on, Jack,
fly on

Declension

"Looking for goshawks is like looking for grace: it comes, but not very often"
– Helen Macdonald

legendary no-nonsense marauder
with harsh guidebook vocabulary:
"ferocity," "irruptive," "ignoble"
hard-bitten nicknames and epithets:
"street brawler" and "cook's friend"
familiar distinctive eye markings:
"blood red eye" or "black eye patch"
harrowing stories centered solely
on its predatory "killing reflex," its
signature "tenacity in pursuit of prey"

banders don't send them up for show;
does not that alone reveal something?
goshawks favor hares and grouse, their
occasional scarcity saying another thing;
we all want a glimpse of this bird, but
glimpses, like some truths, come harder
if two more guidebook epithets now
get factored in: "secretive" the easier,
"depleted" the more difficult and dire

For the Nestlings

Geography Lesson

From Idaho and Iowa, Ontario and Florida
Come bird nerds and photographers
And scores of videographers.

From Delaware and Michigan, these birders get their wish again
They bring great motivation
To see raptors in migration.

Some guy from Wisco just arrived and says he hopes he's not deprived
Of one more opportunity
To bird with this community.

Folks up here from New Orleans in flannel shirts and comfy jeans;
They know our birds, the raptor stuff,
Their life lists, though, aren't full enough!

Some counters come from states out West and bring with them a ton of zest!
Across five states they gamely drive
And tell us tales when they arrive.

Birders here from Illinois leave their count sites for our joy.
Sheridan, Lost Mound, Willow Hill
And four more boast of counting's thrill.

Two pals from Memphis, Tennessee chose to come for Season Three.
They stayed together right downtown;
And hardly ever wore a frown!

They come from Maine and both Dakotas; the best hawk count is Minnesota's.
Of raptor kinds, we've seventeen;
More handsome birds you've never seen.

The Colorado group is here, and Michigan's are drawing near,
So grab your binos and your lunch;
You'll see a lot, I've got a hunch.

Study a weekend's license plates to understand how many states
Have come to Hawk Ridge from afar
And prove how fortunate we are!

Flying Ichabods

One day I heard the flying Ichabods
Better known as the sandhill cranes:
Long necks in front and longer legs behind
Squawking their way to midwestern plains.

Their characteristic clanking sounds bizarre
Whether you're up close or far off.
Sounds like they are gargling metal
Or an alien's horrible cough.

Starting in March, the sandhill cranes converge
In Nebraska on the River Platte.
For six weeks, they are loading up on corn,
Then they fly north when they're good and fat.

The Sleepy Hollow Ichabod's named Crane,
A teacher with a funny face;
But, while on land cranes might look quite strange,
In the sky, they are full of grace.

If you think what you're hearing is honking
But you know it isn't from geese,
Grab your binos and bird book; start studying,
Your knowledge of cranes to increase.

So, next time you are watching for hawks
And hear noisy squawks in the sky,
Look for a string of slender birds up above,
And listen while the sandhill cranes fly by.

Now Playing Right Field
– remembering Kirby, the Kestrel

among the improbable places where American Kestrels might appear,
ballparks are up there with parking ramps, shopping malls, construction sites;
but Kirby, the Kestrel had no problem with improbability on Thursday, May 6, 2010
at Target Field where, in a steady and penetrating drizzle, the first place Minnesota Twins
had failed to score any runs against the last place Baltimore Orioles who'd already scored two runs
and where, in a spectacularly valiant effort to show the hometown team how to use their killer instinct
to dispatch the Orioles as he did moths, this brave, hungry Falco sparverius became an overnight sensation

vivid to this very day—in my memory and on YouTube

our boys had stranded ten teammates, going 0-for-4 with men in scoring position
but by the ninth inning, none of that mattered; Kirby was putting on a show for the ages
he had us in the palm, er – in the feathers of his wings with figure eights and loop-de-loops
up in the sheen and sparkle of the spring mist catching moths above the luminous right field foul pole;
seeing nothing to cheer for down there on the diamond, we turned our eyes instead up into the night sky
riveting them on Kirby's brilliant aerial displays, and don't you know, he made the most of it bringing moths,
one-by-one, back to the yellow pole to eat, to bask in the cheering, and to shake the rainwater off of his wings

and he stays up there showing off—in my memory and on YouTube

next day, he was the lead story on the morning news, on Sports Center, on talk shows,
his name awarded in honor of legendary hometown fielder of days gone by, Kirby Puckett,
who chased flies in centerfield with the same airy acumen we now saw in this new avian avatar,
and while hundreds of kestrels migrate through Hawk Ridge from early September to mid-October,
the closest thing to a foul pole there should probably be referred to, instead, as an owl pole, a decoy owl
on a tall metal pole once used to coax hungry hawks to fly close though it is neither yellow nor illuminated;
experts at Hawk Ridge tell us hawks rarely fly when it rains; now, when you finally get home from Hawk Ridge

for Kirby to fly through the rain and into your memory—make sure to watch him on YouTube

Tweet, Chip, Meow
– a story of the season

Little Sir White-Throat rests on a nearby twig
Tweeting so shrilly from way down on the ground.
Chippy, the chipmunk, hardly gives a fig,
His cheeks being full of seeds he has found.

As if to top both the tweet and the chip,
Lady Catbird flits in meowing her disdain.
She's preparing to start on her long trip
Yet wishing all the while she could remain!

Chippy himself has no plans to migrate,
To head south, to bolt the frigid winter.
Instead, he's making plans to hibernate
Inside the burrow he will soon enter.

Lady C meows to sooth Chippy's distress:
"So sorry migration takes us away!
Wish Hawk Ridge could be our year-long address,
But when the food's gone, we simply can't stay."

Meanwhile, White-Throat's showing off his cool cap,
A tri-colored top, when all's said and done:
Two yellow patches and broad white chin strap,
Two black stripes on both sides of a white one.

Sir White-Throat chimes in to help make it clear
That the best chance for these two to survive
Is, before the winter harshness draws near,
To fly south and ensure staying alive.

"You scamper back and forth across this road,
Your little tail held straight up in the air,
With your cheeks full of seed; Lord, what a load!
Meanwhile, for our trip south we must prepare."

These voices sound from the understory:
White-Throat's shrill call, the catbird's mimic song,
Chippy's squeaks: they are part of the glory
Of fall at Hawk Ridge; it's not here for long!

A Day on My Rock

It's ten o'clock, and I'm now on my rock.
What miracles will there be today?
Scores of Blue Jays in an excited flock;
Cedar Waxwings flying by at play.

Eleven o'clock: yes, I'm on my rock
And the sharp-shins are in the sky.
If Bald Eagles don't come, 'twould be a shock;
Counters say they'll be here by and by.

I jump up now to go watch a release
Where Allie holds up a harrier.
Banded and airborne, its freedom increased;
Watching this, I'm feeling merrier!

It's twelve o'clock high; my rock I'm still on,
But a stretch and a break I need now.
I'll talk with Margie and say hi to John,
Then finish my break with some chow.

It's now one o'clock; I'm back on my rock,
The broad wings are kettling above.
They're climbing higher which is really no shock:
Soon, they'll stream which I am fond of.

I'm sleepy, it's two; I'm yet on my rock.
It's like I've been here forever!
Clinton's talking now; he's here 'round the clock.
For a bird nerd, he really is clever.

It's three, and I'm just now leaving my rock
When John yells out, "Hey! Swainson's Hawk!"
The birders stand on the street chock-a-block;
This rare sighting stops all the talk.

Four o'clock, at last, and I've left my rock.
I'll drive home by way of the bridge.
I'll be back tomorrow for sure; it's a lock.
The fun never stops at Hawk Ridge!

The Falcon Box

Every spring, Peregrine Falcons return to nesting boxes on tall buildings, cliffs, and bluffs. Hawk Ridge Bird Observatory once had a Peregrine Watch program in downtown Duluth. The nesting box is still there. This poem is about a nesting pair of Peregrine Falcons and their three chicks in the spring of 2018.

A female Peregrine Falcon on a gravel nest
In a box two-hundred ten feet in the air.
Parents and eggs both face a stern test;
Already three weeks they've been there.

The guard is now changing at the door;
The male makes sure the eggs are turned.
He settles down atop the brown eggs four,
And Mom gets the break she has earned.

The female's much bigger than her mate;
Of that fact we can always be sure.
Males and females both dutifully wait;
Rain, wind, even snow they'll endure.

Most Peregrine Falcons pair up for life
And fly back North each year to raise
Three or four chicks despite all the strife
Of guarding eggs for thirty-five days.

When time is right, the eggs will hatch;
Toward daylight the hatchlings soon hop.
Helpless and blind, they cannot yet catch
Any food, so their parents must "shop."

Each chick's no more than a little fuzz ball;
They mature in their nest rather fast,
And soon the instinct to migrate will call;
Safe days in the nest do not last.

In long autumn shadows of September,
Falcon fledglings finally move out,
And before long, they do not remember
What life in the box was about.

Wintry weather helps them to determine
When it's time to leave the nest shelf;
A peregrine's life's a good sermon:
You'll just have to watch for yourself.

A Quartet of Quartets

Falco Peregrinus

After the experience at Hawk Ridge recalled in the opening poem in Dramatis Personae (p. 48), I wanted to learn more about the family life of Peregrine Falcons, their amazing comeback from near-extinction, and their peerless skill as hunters. From April 15 to July 1 of 2018, I spent several minutes a day watching a nesting pair of peregrines through a DNR webcam inside a nesting box 200 feet off the ground on the side of the Bremer Bank Building in St. Paul, Minnesota. The box faces east, and the camera is at the back. Four eggs appeared on April 9 only three of which actually hatched. I last saw all three nestlings in the box a week past the summer solstice.

Peregrine Cam

I watch the nest
at sundown
the female falcon
watching me watch her
or so it seems
she is quite still now
as are her two chicks
with two remaining eggs
a tableau in egg shells,
feathers, and hatchling down
blowing about
small eyes blinking
beaks yawning
the steady silent
rhythmic breathing
of eons

Cam Medley

rag doll heads on spastic torsos
face down each in its own corner
three flattened Oreo cookies asleep
barely a breath, blink or heartbeat

in the next minute twitching
bumping and careening about
the poop-stained nesting box
nudging each other to the back

the trio of fuzzy pantalooned
suppliants await delivery
of the next in an endless
series of avian sacrifices

staring out into daylight like
three white-and-slate flecked
stuffed birds awaiting homes
statuesque triplets at the edge

no clue how or even whether
to cope with the ungainly things
attached to their shoulders
as yet too inept for the inevitable test drive

First Flight

Oh, peregrine chick alone on the brink
What do your sharp eyes watch so intently
There on the threshold of your next life?
Your sibling has already tested her wings,
Left the wooden confines of your nursery,
Left you to take that next step on your own.

You follow something with your eyes, now;
It must be her, the bolder one, the older one,
For whom this next frightful step came easily,
As if an immense magnet had pulled her off,
Forced her up and out into a new wider world,
As if she'd heard whispers saying "now is the time."

She has returned to escape the morning rain,
Shake off her feathers, tell you of the ease and thrill,
The leaving and returning, how simply wondrous,
And the freedom, how much to see beyond the box.
Over and over, you step up to the edge and look out,
Eyeing a waking world, and then think better of it.

Gone, But . . .

earth-brown ovals in a dusting of April snow
impossible, then, to see them as handsome
perched sentinels, much less riding the wind

helpless and haphazard white fuzz balls gawk
sprawl about with impatient gaping beaks
demanding ever more sinew guts or shreds

three downy clowns bobbing around the box
doing face plants and flapping the awkward
and crooked devices on their hunched backs

crowded squawking trio, bumping into walls,
into their mother and each other, now darker
and with longer feathers but still ungainly feet

asleep in neutral corners amid whitewash,
wing parts, gooey leftovers, and not-yet
realized, partially-formed dreams of flight

teetering on a variety of ersatz launchpads
sudden bursts of random practice wingbeats
flapping about prepping for eventual liftoff

I imagine them yelling "Look out, you two!"
or *"So that's* how these weird things work!"
or just "No, *you* go first! C'mon, I *dare* you!"

brightened by a June morning's brilliant light,
the box with its open front is vacant and lifeless,
its feather-strewn inside lacks any raison d'etre

scarcely a week into joining yet another stream
of robust and hungry Falco peregrinus fledglings,
the nest's charismatic trio has departed for good

they will not return, like much in this humble life,
but they're in my mind, one alone or all three together
with confident wingbeats heedless of any farewell

Full Disclosure
– for Steve Kolbe

This quartet concerns the Common Nighthawk, a member of the nightjar (Caprimulgidae) family. Full disclosure: they are not hawks. They do migrate, however, in vast numbers down along Lake Superior's northern coast only for a little more than two weeks in early autumn. Occasionally, they veer inland enough to reach Hawk Ridge in their purposeful, early, and often wildly frenetic rush to Central and South America.

First Day, 9/1/18

    the blue
the welcoming blue
it mesmerizes you
or it will if you let it
    and when you do,
out of the white-flecked vastness
will come such wonders

like now
today, the first day
by the scores they come
these nighthawks
    turned day hawks
swirl and twist and spin
    a bent-winged swarm
    a stream of whirligigs
the drift and swoop of it all
    right there
    first above us
then
over there
    higher in the deep blue
out over the lake's own blue
    a feathered whirlwind
    myriad wingbeats
    all perfect
    in their evening ecstasy
    all perfect in ours

Forget the Binos!

"Oh, my God! Dude, look! Up there! And forget the binos!"
you hear yourself say as the wingbeat dream begins; just
lean back: you're under a tsunami of striped boomerangs

watching the crook and veer above, you reach up toward it,
toward the hellbent purposeful feathered drive and the sheer
incalculable, the dizzying and flapping maelstrom overhead

laugh out loud when Steve shouts, "*That* was five hundred!"
you know an estimate when you hear one, but truthfully
you do not know a thing anymore under this nightjar storm

each one is a winged hypnotist daring you to wake up,
to count it, to stay alert distinguishing, as Steve and the experts do,
their flight pattern and behavior, noting their shape and color

you want to escape, to forget being anchored on the brick patio
compelled by the magnetic tug of such a twilight spectacle;
he continues to bark out numbers that mean nothing at all to you

the birds are flying into a salmon-shaded sunset; you have lost focus
every one you try to watch diminishes in its own private instant
and joins the ecstatic receding procession, a turbulent river of wings

the forgotten binoculars hang limp and useless; the last few birds
have long since passed overhead, their dark pandemonium gone,
and you, you are nowhere near waking from a wild nighthawk dream

Chevron Wings

it is their name that unlocks
    these pictures
        and the name is the key
            nighthawks . . .

dimly in the fog
of decades hard upon one another
out on the hillside east of home
four little footloose boys
running in summer's dank dusk
above them are the mysterious peents and booms
listen, Dad says:
listen to the nighthawks
no, no such thing as too many
    they eat mosquitos
        you hear that sound, boys?
            listen, listen to that

ahead a quarter-century, and now
the ballplayers are hard at work, at play on groomed grass
the smell of tobacco permeates
a sixty-year old urban minor league ballpark
and chevron-winged nightjars feast
on clouds of moths circling the bright lights
the endless darting aerial dance
watch the flapping and listen to the whoosh
above the crack of the bat
and the slap of leather
    summer sights
        summer sounds
           summertime baseball dream

on a rooftop patio here, tonight
wild wingbeats herald the nighthawks
pounding low through the lakeside twilight
again, the chevron wings pushing them southwest
flocks of nighthawks twenty fifty a hundred
streaming toward the quarter-moon
into the pastel orange and fading blue of dusk
flap and glide across miles, along through time
through sounds and smells
    the ancient ritual
        come tomorrow night, he says:
           they will be here again

Just Specks

pointing out threads of birds
streaming above the ridge
John says they're just specks
he counts them as we watch
enters the final number
mechanically, as he must

I try to think of each bird,
each dusky nighthawk, as a
speck in a continuous line
stretching back down time
back before the cataclysm
sixty-seven point four mya
following the seasons with
its precious genetic code

think of each flighted speck
from origin to destination
think of the fraught journey
these specks more unique
than identical in the stream
like all of us here watching

I Shall Be Released

Release I

after your sudden capture
we hold you for mere minutes
that's all, Red-tail, and we
promise no delay beyond this:

just an aluminum ring
its runic scribbling
irrelevant to your
own migrant soar;
then to be held up
like an ice-cream cone
while we gawk at the pierce
of your fixed yellow stare
entranced by your liquid neck;

before you are raised up
time for just a glimpse
under the miracle that is
the gentle beige order
of your sweet feathered wing
some vaguely critical statistics
merely an etcetera beyond
the geography of your vast itinerary;
then the careful transfer
a new hand, its grasp
filled with electric expectancy;
then the onetwothree,
and just as you are set free
the thrill runs through us all

we borrow a brief stay, Red-tail,
enforce a captive instant
just for that and to see
the nearness of your
confident wingbeats
southward down the ridge
while we in our own captivity
shout or clap or wave
and choke back the moist
and silent tears of envy

Release II

hardly twins, the pair of roughies
on the final morning of October
both dark, the male much smaller

their double descent now causes
a palpable stir in the congregation
we are spellbound by the twosome

materializing without abracadabra
their mesmerizingly shaggy legs
the brown spell of their soft wings

creating a buzz as if the handlers
had just pulled them out of a top hat
still star-struck, I choose the bigger,

my eager fingers reach toward it
like blossoms welcoming sunlight
I hold up its sublime weightlessness

a brown cloudlet which, at the moment
of release, lifts effortlessly noiselessly
regaining freedom more than altitude

Release III

like you are
holding a cup
he tells me
my eyes intent
like the hawk's
make a C now
its head turns
miraculously
they can do that
close your fingers
around mine
wildness in our hands
bony yellow legs
long talons stretch
hold him up
we all watch
hawk and people
all quiet now
its brown streaks
radiate a dark wild
instructions again
hold him up
like The Statue
of Liberty
perfect images
cup and statue
held high
one two three
and, yes
liberty

Andy and the Sharpie

two steps up the worn crosstie stairs
raise the borrowed migrant one-fisted
wave this yellow-eyed youngster
and ask for a guess or two
cameras and cell phones rise as one
the bird looks back at you
as if its identity should be obvious
peregrine: no
Cooper's Hawk: again, no
you affirm the third guess:
yes, you say: Sharp-shinned Hawk

you ask how we know
once more it spins its protective head
gives you its flinty admonition
not exactly impatient but ready
more than ready to rejoin the wind
your fingers draw its stare back out
feature the deep brown belly streaks
show us its dark back
the weapons its talons are
talk up the bony tarsometatarsus

who has never released one, you ask, and
goaded by her dad, a youngster steps up
which hand? right? okay now make a C
      hold it like a cone
            on the count of three
                  lift it up high and
                        open your hands
a few quick flaps up and a swerve overhead
low over the shrubs it seeks its former path
deaf to clapping, yays, woo-hoos, and sighs;
we are abandoned by another banded escapee
your earnest pitch now merely background to the sense
that, less for the hawk than for us, it was all over too soon

All Things Must Pass

Perspective

why
you ask
why spend so much effort and time there
on hawks and eagles
      on vultures, ravens
      falcons, even crows,
           crows, for goodness sake?
why, when the climate is changing
      families are struggling
      and nations are warring?
why, when incomes are dwindling
      costs are running higher
      resources are getting scarcer
      and infrastructure is crumbling?
why these raptors, now, of all things?

I echo the inquiry slowly: why?
      why? I say once more
I will tell you why, so, listen up:
for thousands of years
      hundreds of thousands of years
      millions of years, to be more precise
they do what is best for their species
what ensures their survival
      guarantees food and safety for their young
         makes certain that the family endures
            through stress and upheaval
they do what maximizes the chances for positive outcomes
      they do what minimizes the chances for negative ones
they live their short miraculous migratory lives
      every minute of every day
         doing what is best for their species
not what is worst

The Season's Last Bald

nice adult bald there John says calmly;
vague disinterest follows, no one speaks
the gray sky reflects our quiet listlessness,
it leaches relentlessly into the last of us,
figures in slow motion wearing the day
like it was a sodden, heavy woolen blanket

I raise my binoculars more to be seeing
less gray than to locate the laggard bird;
my reward is a short search and a full view,
a chance burst of sunlight catches the eagle
looking from side to side circling lazily above,
its white head studying its spellbound studiers

flaplessly the majestic bird banks sunward
capturing the momentary morning shaft
glinting off the white head and tail feathers,
and glinting into me is the bird's purity, its
freedom translated into an inherent nobility
that stretches beyond today and beyond time

Closing Time

The chickadees are finally the stars of the show again, but that's the last of the black oil seed, for sure. Funny, I could have sworn I saw one more bag of it under the observation deck just a day or two ago. It's going to be slim pickings up here pretty soon.

What will I miss most when the snow flies? It's a toss-up: Pringles cans, kettles, certain voices, certain smiles, that whole release thing is so spellbinding, too. And the view never disappoints. Ever.

Highlights? Just one, really: rarely failing to come away with a poem even when it appears that absolutely nothing is happening. It's strange reflecting on how fast three months go by. It's even stranger to be zipping up my jacket now instead of lifting up my binoculars.

Weird. It seems like only yesterday . . .

November

"Hey, now, hey, now, don't dream it's over." – Crowded House

There is no long line of cars parked up here anymore. No license plates from Ohio, Oregon or Ontario. Wasn't it just a few days ago when the colors were so magnificent? What a time that was.

Ishmael comes to mind again now that November has arrived. Seabirds were more his thing. And whales. Not many seabirds at Hawk Ridge, much less whales. My coffee loses its heat a lot faster these days. I wish I knew where the little blue darter I released in September finally wound up. I'm guessing Jack still has a long way to go to get to the Ozarks.

Stephen does not have much company up here nowadays. Last Tuesday was definitely the right day to take him a pizza. I'm cold. Before I even raised the shades this morning, I heard my neighbor shoveling his driveway.

Glossary

Archaeopteryx - 150-million year old ancestor of modern birds found in what is now southern Germany

binos - shorthand for binoculars

blue darter - a nickname given to several species of raptors, most commonly to Sharp-shinned Hawks

cere - a soft waxy, fleshy often yellow covering at the base of the upper beak in birds of prey

corvid - a member of the Corvidae family of 120 species of birds that include ravens, crows and jays

cynosure - paragon or apogee; model; highest or purest form of

diabase - an igneous rock compositionally equivalent to basalt; rock formations underlying Hawk Ridge

dihedral - in a slightly or (in the case of Turkey Vultures) noticeably upward, V-shaped wing position

grok - to understand fully, to drink, to become one with; coined by writer Robert A. Heinlein in 1961

leucistic - mostly white due to loss of or partial pigmentation; not to be confused with albino

mya - accepted shorthand among paleontologists for a "million years ago"

parallax - the effect of an object's appearance changing when viewed from different positions

peents - short, two-syllable nasal buzzing sounds; may sound more like "bee-ent" or "beee-ownt"

Pleistocene - period of time between 2.6 mya to twelve thousand years ago; an era of repeated glaciation

pterosaurs - cousins of the therapods; in their heyday, many were soaring giants with colorful crests

roughies - nickname for Rough-legged Hawks

Swarovskis - high-end binoculars and spotting scopes; frequently seen on the Hawk Ridge observation platform

Tenochtitlan - 14th-Century mega-city in Mexico, center of the Aztec civilization until Spanish conquest

therapods - dinosaurs; the true prehistoric ancestors of modern birds; distant cousins of pterosaurs

Acknowledgments

My brothers—Jim, John, and Charlie—are accomplished naturalists who have dedicated most of their professional lives in one way or another to the study and preservation of the planet's wondrous biodiversity and wild habitat. Since forever ago, their work and their passion for the natural world has inspired me. With this book, I am delighted to add to our family's long-standing commitment to reaching and teaching audiences large and small about wildlife, natural history, and habitat, our own as well as that of the birds. With every family I watch at Hawk Ridge, I hear echoes of our parents gently, passionately ushering the four of us ever more deeply into the world of birds.

One of the greatest pleasures in the process of completing this project has been getting to know Jan and John Green. According to my brothers, who started seeing Jan at Minnesota Ornithologists' Union meetings down in the Twin Cities in the 60s, she is a legend among Minnesota birders. As members of the Superior Hiking Trail Association, Jan and John took the lead long ago in designing and then cutting trails around the overlook at Hawk Ridge to broaden its appeal and increase access to the raptors' migratory path. Jan continues to work on, write about, and advocate for Minnesota's birds. I have relished my time with the Greens. I am grateful for their stories from the early years at Hawk Ridge, the wealth of articles and photographs they have shared with me about a half-century of birding and geologic study in Duluth, and for their unflagging interest in and support of this book.

It's risky for a poet to solicit suggestions from potential readers in advance of his book's publication. A poet's choices about syntax, imagery, format, and construction should theoretically remain his or her own. I have been particularly fortunate, however, to have friends who were more than willing to double check my writing not just for the obvious errors, of which I can be counted on to make many, but for the subtle, nuanced, and camouflaged ones as well. Thanks to Elizabeth Hunter, Marna Banks, and Dan D'Allaird for their time and reliably thoughtful suggestions. I am also indebted to Jeanne Filiatrault Laine for her insightful final read-through of the manuscript. And a very special thanks to Mike Savage who took it upon himself to do much more for the book than simply to publish it. The pleasure of working with him for the better part of two years has been surpassed only by the delight in becoming friends.

It would have been virtually impossible to finish without the wisdom and perspective of my writing group. To receive comments from other poets is especially rewarding in this process, and so I'd like to thank Ellie Schoenfeld, Deb Cooper, Candace Ginsberg, and Penny Perry. They offer their insights thoughtfully, creatively, and always with kindness and humor.

I am at great pains to find words to express how important and inspired Mikayla Haynes's videography was in the early stages of developing the Kickstarter Campaign for the book. She was sensitive to the demands of capturing the essence of Hawk Ridge, and her vision of what an introductory five-minute video should look like was invaluable in helping me to clarify for myself what the book might eventually look like.

Here in Duluth, the community of poets is enthusiastic, talented and constantly growing. From it, I have taken much inspiration. There are countless collections of poems written over the years by a prodigious number of poets of stature whose breadth of experience and clarity of insight make our city both a haven and a mecca for aspiring poets. I am thankful to be surrounded by so many accessible, prolific, and generous writers. The Poet Laureate program begun in 2006 by Jim Perlman of Lake Superior Writers and Holy Cow Press is an ongoing testament to the city's commitment to honoring writing of all kinds. The half-dozen or more public poetry readings scheduled annually are only the most visible ways in which Duluth shares its rich mother lode of talent with an increasingly receptive and supportive audience. I am deeply grateful for the lengthening list of thoughtful, creative, and dedicated writers of poetry here.

Many thanks to Jeff Frey and Kelly McFaul-Solem at CPL for their patience and inspired graphics work. I am so very grateful to Jan Bustrak and Jill Johnson for their professional and supportive editing and design assistance. I am much happier, and the book is much better for their enthusiastic involvement. Mike Savage is the consummate professional as a publisher. I will always be grateful for his commitment to and support of this project from the outset.

The staff members of the Hawk Ridge Bird Observatory are dedicated, knowledgeable, and generous. I appreciate every moment of their steadfast assistance. Thanks to Janelle Long, Margie Menzies, Clinton Nienhaus, John Richardson, Frank Nicoletti, Stephen Nelson, and Steve Kolbe for their help and cooperation. In addition, I received much encouragement from Noel Larson, Hannah Toutonghi, Kaitlyn Okrusch, Allie Quick, Andy Witchger, and Alex Sundvall. Whether in shorts and sandals or parkas and boots, these gentle, industrious and passionate new friends were an inspiration to me every day that I watched and wrote alongside them as they did their work. I am also grateful to have made the acquaintance of and received information about Hawk Ridge from Bruce Munson, Larry Snyder, Larry and Jan Kramer, and Gene and Susan Bauer. Profuse thanks to Ann Klefstad, Laura Erickson, and Bart Sutter for taking time to offer their kind testimonials for the back cover of the book. I am grateful beyond measure to Dyana Furmansky for her Foreword and even more for her important book about the life of Rosalie Edge. No one could have been more right than Ms. Edge for rescuing raptors from the scourge of sport shooting in the 1930s, and no writer could have done a better job than Ms. Furmansky not only of making Edge's life and work accessible but of revealing its exemplary quality.

My college classmate and dear friend Elizabeth Hunter has been watching hawks for decades at Rockfish Gap in Virginia, at Cape May, New Jersey, and now at Hawk Ridge. Without her inspiration and encouragement over the past two years, it would never have occurred to me to write these poems let alone put them into a book. She has an ornithologist's skill at identification, an artist's ability to see things others don't see, and a poet's eye for detail and command of language. Her enthusiasm for migration is boundless whether it be of raptors, sandhill cranes, monarch butterflies, or humpback whales.

How foolish my original plan looks now to use photographs to illustrate these poems. Photos of raptors come a dime-a-dozen, no slight intended to the many talented, well-equipped, hard-working and prolific photographers at Hawk Ridge. But Penny Perry's drawings are utterly and exquisitely unique. In Mike Savage's words, they are "really sublime." They evoke all that I see and hear and imagine at Hawk Ridge. They are timeless. They breathe a life into these poems that would otherwise have been impossible to achieve. They capture fragility and strength; they render the mystery and the magic of flight. In each drawing can be found some of the grace we are gifted with every time we encounter these birds. I am so grateful for Penny's willingness to collaborate with me and to find such vision in my poetry as these drawings reveal. Her perspective on the wild world and her sensibility as an artist have been an inspiration to me. Whatever success and longevity come to this book would have been quite impossible without the gift of these wonderful drawings.

My heartfelt thanks go out to the many friends, family members, and total strangers who pledged their support for this project. Their generous participation in the Kickstarter Campaign ensured the book's completion. In particular, I wish to thank my aunt Charlotte Brown and my cousin, Dorothy Weaver Podell for their generous support and for their long-standing faith in my writing.

Finally, I'd like to thank my daughter, Courtney. Her own book, *Maji Moto: Dispatches from a Drought,* is a high bar for a writer in any genre, and her life, family and work are the very best kind of poetry.

Bibliography

Ackerman, Jennifer. *The Genius of Birds*. New York: Penguin Books, 2016.

Bildstein, Keith L. *Migrating Raptors of the World: Their Ecology and Conservation*. Ithaca, NY: Comstock Publishing Associates, 2006.

Broun, Maurice. *Hawks Aloft: The Story of Hawk Mountain*. Mechanicsburg, PA: Stackpole Books, 1948.

Brusatte, Steve. *The Rise and Fall of the Dinosaurs: A New History of a Lost World*. New York: William Morrow, 2018.

Conniff, Richard. "Weirdest Wonders on Wings." *National Geographic*. November 2017 60-79.

Dunn, Jon L. and Jonathan Alderfer. *Field Guide to the Birds of North America, 7th Edition*. Washington, D.C.: National Geographic, 2017.

Dunn, Pete with Kevin T. Carlson. *Birds of Prey*. Boston: Houghton Mifflin Harcourt, 2016.

Erickson, Laura. *Hawk Ridge: Minnesota's Birds of Prey*. Minneapolis: University of Minnesota Press, 2012.

Fitzpatrick, C.L. *Maji Moto: Dispatches from a Drought*. Durham, North Carolina: Horse & Buggy Press, 2012.

Franzen, Jonathan. "Why Birds Matter." *National Geographic* January 2018 30-43.

Furmansky, Dyana Z. *Rosalie Edge, Hawk of Mercy: The Activist Who Saved Nature From the Conservationists*. Athens, GA: University of Georgia Press, 2009.

Jaggard, Victoria. "The Dinosaurs That Didn't Die." *National Geographic*. May 2018 78-97.

Kaufman, Kenn. *Kingbird Highway: The Biggest Year in the Life of an Extreme Birder*. New York: Houghton Mifflin Company, 1997.

Liguori, Jerry. *Hawks from Every Angle: How to Identify Raptors in Flight*, Princeton: Princeton University Press, 2005.

Lovette, Irby J. and John W. Fitzpatrick. *The Cornell Lab of Ornithology Handbook of Bird Biology, Third Edition*. Ithaca, NY: Cornell University Press, 2016.

Macdonald, Helen. *H is for Hawk*. New York: Grove Press, 2014.

Tekiela, Stan. *Bird Migration*. Cambridge, MN: Adventure Publications, 2018.

Weidensaul, Scott. *Living on the Wind: Across the Hemisphere with Migratory Birds*. New York: North Point Press, 1999.

Other Poems About Raptors

"Hawk of Mercy" by Rosalie Edge in *Rosalie Edge, Hawk of Mercy* by Dyana Furmansky, 2012

"The Windhover" by Gerard Manley Hopkins in *Poems of Gerard Manley Hopkins*, 1918

"The Night-Hawk" by Dorothy Cooper in *Poetry, A Magazine of Verse* - February 1934

"Evening Hawk" by Robert Penn Warren in *New and Selected Poems, 1923-1985*, 1985

"A Red-tailed Hawk at Home in the World" by Nancy Willard in *The Sea at Truro*, 2012

"Tamer and Hawk" by Thom Gunn in *Selected Poems, 1950-1975*, 1979

"Hurt Hawks" by Robinson Jeffers in *Cawdor and Other Poems*, 1928

"Osprey" by Billy Collins in *Aimless Love*, 2013

"Cascade Raptor Center: Capture" by Andrew Feld in *Raptor*, 2012

"The Hawks" by Ellie Schoenfeld in *Bound Together: Like the Grasses*, 2013

"Hawk Ridge" by Gary Boelhower in *Marrow, Muscle, and Flight*, 2011

"Hawk Ridge" by Jim Johnson in *Yoik*, 2015

"Eagle Poem" by Joy Harjo in *How We Became Human: New and Selected Poems*, 2002

"Hawk in the Rain" by Ted Hughes in *Hawk in the Rain*, 1957

"Between Two Shores" by Sheila Packa in *Trail Guide to the Northland Experience in Prints and Poetry*, 2008

"Sparrow Hawk Resting" by Loren Eiseley in *Another Kind of Autumn*, 1977

"The Hawk" by W.B. Yeats in *The Wild Swans at Coole*, 1919

"Hawk" by Mary Oliver in *New and Selected Poems, Volume 1*, 1992

"Peregrine" by Barton Sutter in *Farewell to the Starlight in Whiskey*, 2004

"The Dalliance of the Eagles" by Walt Whitman in *Leaves of Grass*, 1892

"Of Amplitude There is No Scraping Bottom" by Jane Hirshfield in *The Beauty*, 2015

"To a Farmer Who Hung Five Hawks on His Barbed Wire" by David Wagoner in *Bright Wings*, 2009

"Peregrine Falcon, New York City" by Robert Cording in *Common Life*, 2006

"Widening Circles" by Rainer Maria Rilke in *Book of Hours*, 1905

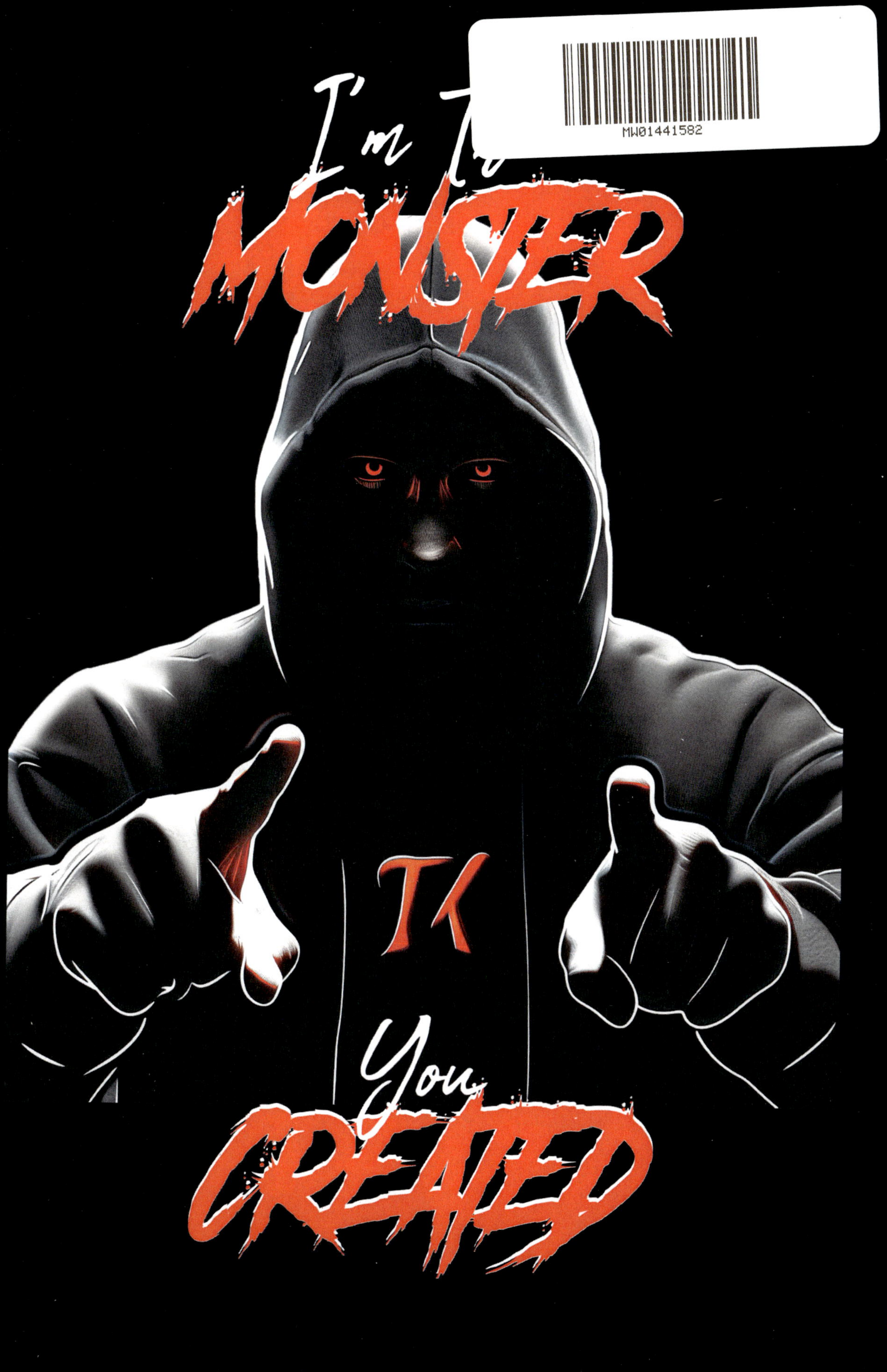

I'm
MONSTER
TK
You
CREATED

https://www.youtube.com/@TKinConTROLL

All rights reserved. Printed and bound in the United States of America. No part of this book may be reproduced or transmitted in any form by any means, electric or mechanical, including photocopying, recording, or by an information storage and retrieval system without permission in writing from the publisher, except by a reviewer, who may quote brief passages in a review. Published by Stamina Enterprise.

Illustration Designs by: Derek Anderson Sr
Writer: Derek Anderson Sr
Editor: Jamie Anderson

ISBN: 979-8-9919737-4-8

For information regarding special discounts for bulk purchases of this book for educational or gift purposes, as a charitable donation, or to arrange a speaking event with the author, please contact: info@TKinControll.com

Copyright© 2025, Derek Anderson Sr.

Team Wolf

Be ready on my Signal.

YAAHHH..
YAAHHH..
BANG..
BANG..

Congratulations on being a hero to our country Major Saban Scott
Man I miss the good old days of kicking bad people's ass.
What's for breakfast dad?
Your favorite as always

Panel 1:
- Dad, can i be home schooled ?
- Oh no ma'am ! Home school dosen't teach you how to interact with other people.

Panel 2:
- We'll can I transfer schools beacause I don't like those people there?
- Tiffanty, you can't run from every situation just because you don't mine a few poeple.

Panel 3:
- I'm sorry ! let's talk about it more tomorrow.
- Ugh...I knew you wouldn't understand ! just forget it.

I hate these trolls!

I can't take it anymore. These trolls won't stop!

I can't believe they did this to my daughter!

They will pay.

All of them.

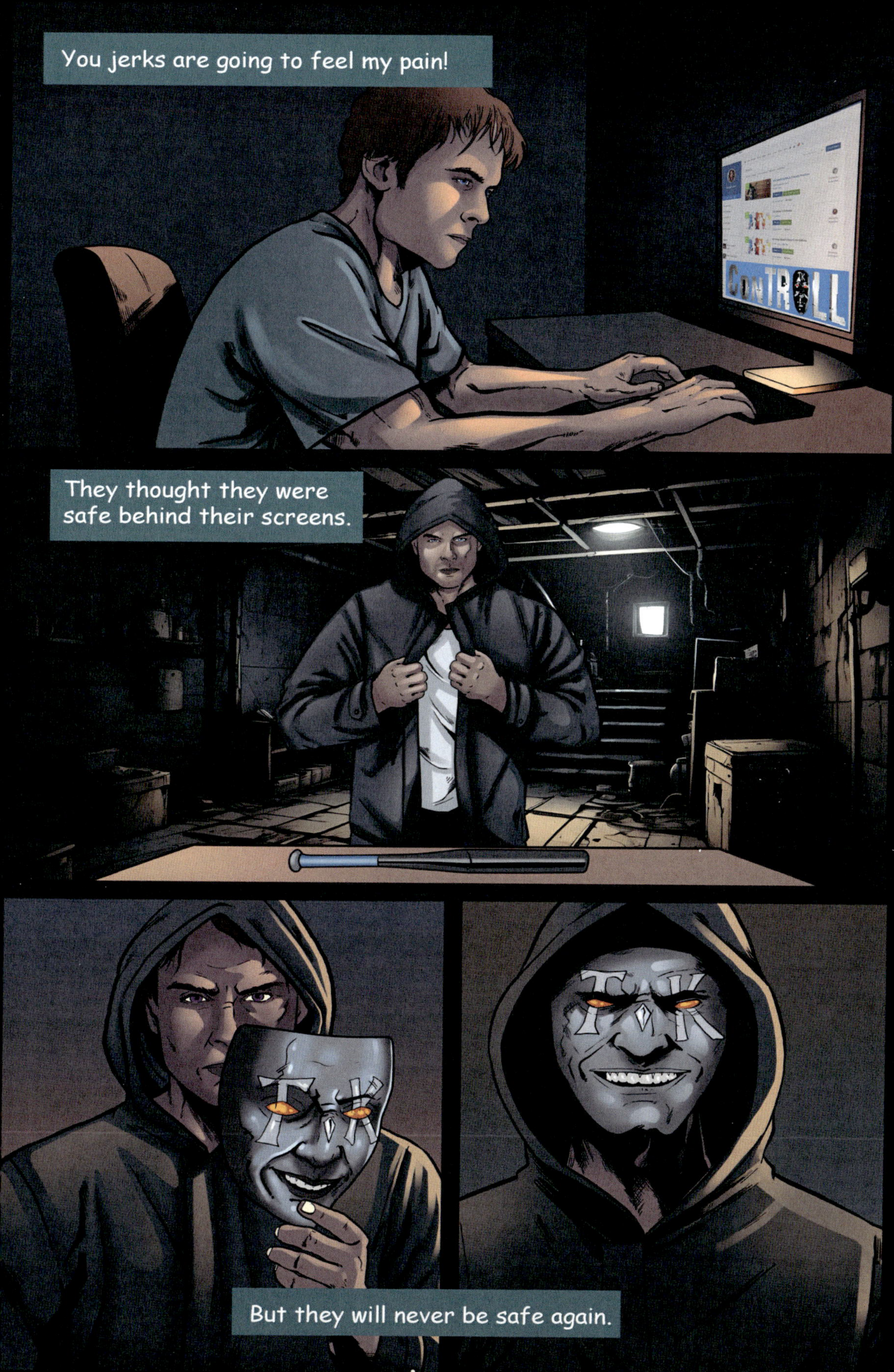

These Trolls are always hiding, but I'm going to find you ALL.
ConTROLL
W-wait... please...
Don't cry now you Coward!
Justice isn't coming....But I AM

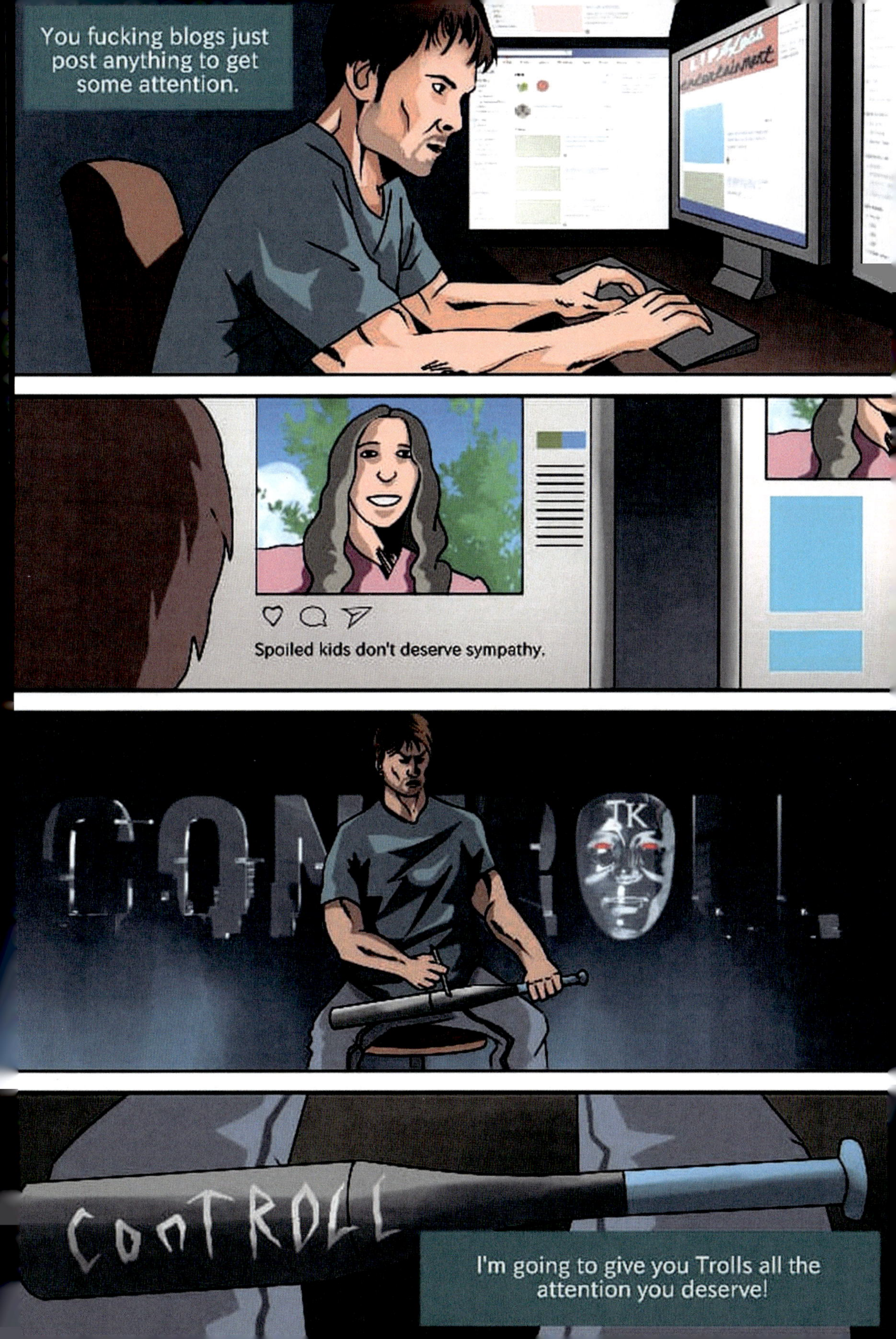
You fucking blogs just post anything to get some attention.
Spoiled kids don't deserve sympathy.
CONTROLL
I'm going to give you Trolls all the attention you deserve!

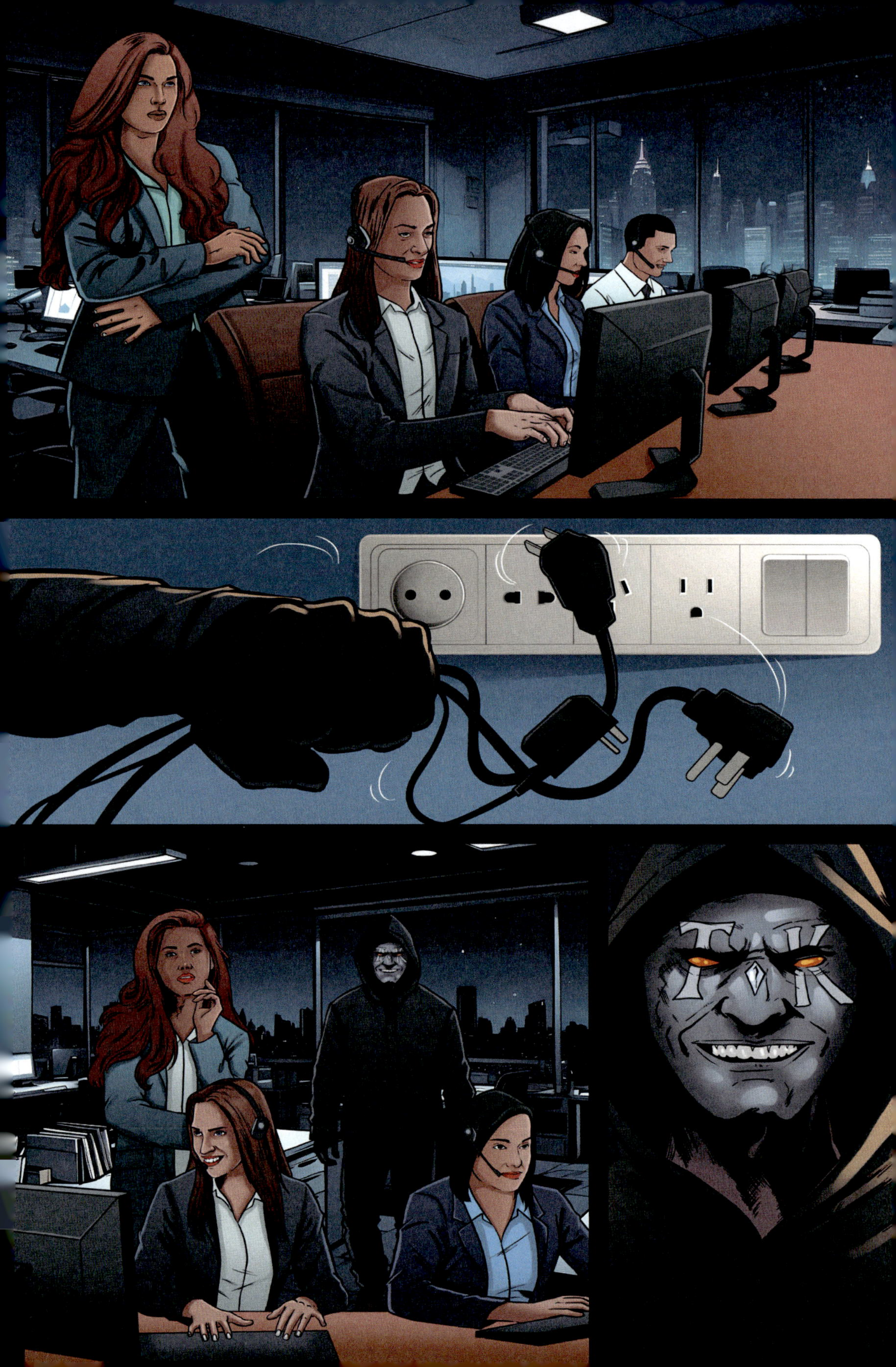

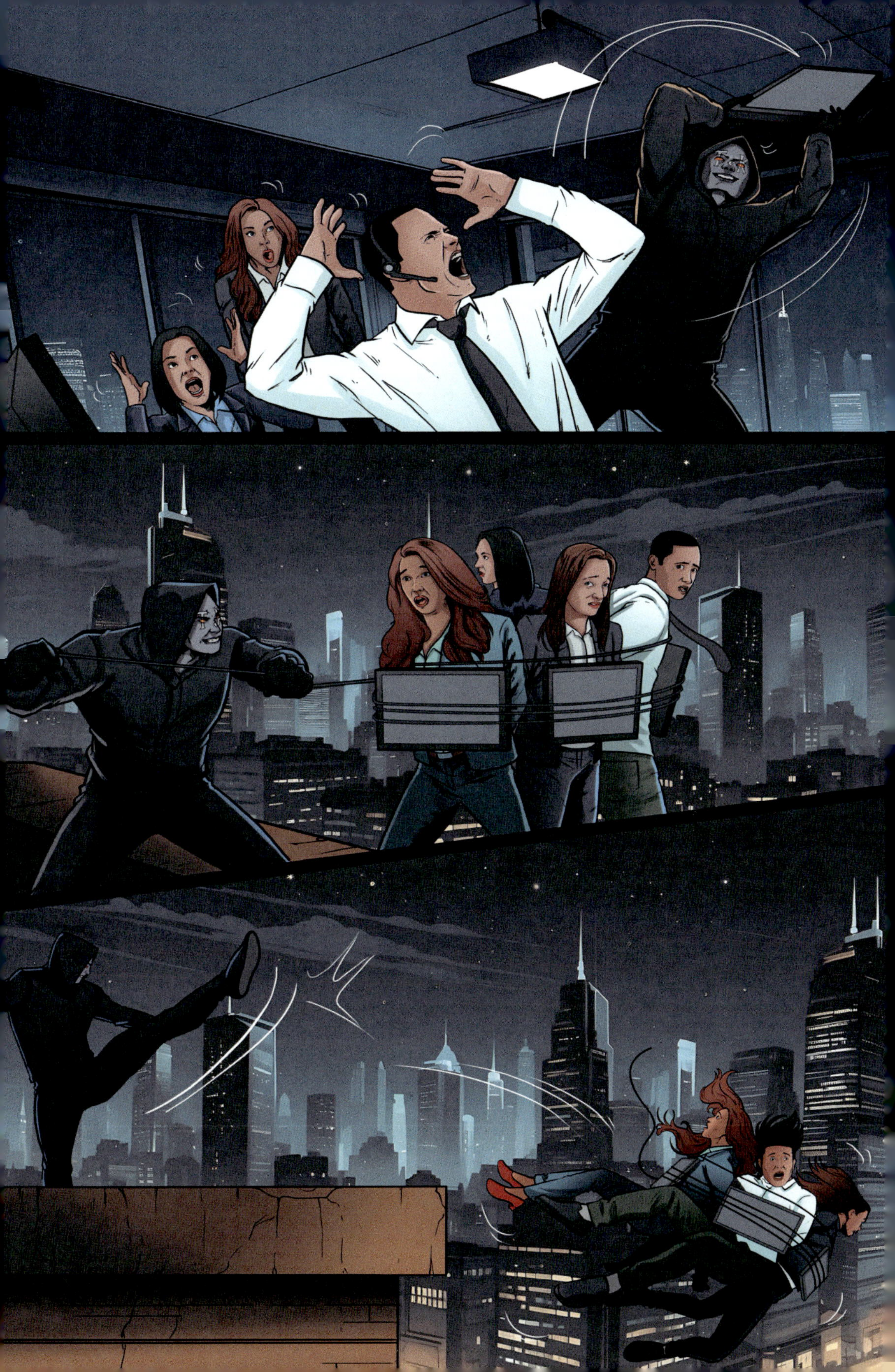

YOU BLOG SITES ARE ABOUT TO GET THE MISERY YOU PUT OUT!
TK HATES YOU GOSSIPING TROLLS

These kids were not her friends at all.
These kids are so mean to each other !
You aren't cute like us so stop trying!
I see they need to be controlled just like the adults !

OH IT'S THESE TWO TROUBLE MAKERS!

LET 'EM HANG LONGER

IT'S LIKE LIVE-ACTION KARMA

TALK ABOUT A PUBLIC SERVICE ANNOUNCEMENT!

THE TROLL KING LEAVES HIS MARK

GIVE THEM A LITTE LONGER TO THINK ABOUT THIS KARMA THEY'RE GETTING
SHOULD I CALL 911 YET?
TK
TK
I'm A Troll
I'm A
I HOPE THIS TEACHES THEM TO STOP TROLLING!
CENTRAL HIGH SCHOOL
I HOPE IT TEACHES ALL OF THEM TO STOP TROLLING!
EVERYONE GO BACK TO CLASS!

You guys don't have to be jerks just because you're losing.
Shut your punk azz up!
Right or we will choke you with your own cord!
Yeah and you better not let us see you outside!
You kids talk way too much shit!
PAF..
HA..HA..HA..!
Stop being jerks and just play the Game!

Thank you for meeting up with me Greg.
It's good to see you man! I miss my Team Wolf brothers!
HOORAY!
Do you find it hard dealing with this new world
This new world isn't much different then the one we grew up in.
Naw man. We had respect for other people even if we didn't agree with them.
Yeah but some people don't have self respect so it's hard for them to understand.
I wish I would have listened to you Tiffany! And I wish I was with you
Tiffany Scott
But I have to get rid of these social media clowns once and for-all.

LIVE

I'm the Only King.

I told y'all I'm the new king of social media.

No one cares how much money you have or how cute your kids are.

LIVE

AAAAHHH....

Let's see how many so called celebrities I can piss off today!
CHEESE
BISTRO
I hate you fuckin fans more than Some of these asshole celebrities!
TROLL KILLER
BAM..
TROLL KILLER
LIVE
You Trolls don't deserve jail time...
You deserve the same pain you put out!

My ex is a piece of shit so don't y'all date him!
Ima make sure he's Never happy!
I'm going to stalk her until she comes back to me!
I'll make sure you don't see him happy!
I'm stalking you stalkers!

YOU WANT A FIGHT
I WANT A WAR

How do we know how many people he's hurt?
And this makes his 10th victim
All of them have the initials T.K. On their face!
The crazy part is he has his own Social Media Pages.
We've been trying but he uses the dark web to hide and then deletes everything before we can catch him.
Then just track his IP address and find this killer!
I'll stay on his page and keep trying to get it shut down
I don't know if I should arrest him or tell him Thank you

Why are you so caught up in this Troll Guy?

You mean TK the hero?

So when did killing people become heroic?

Every sense he's stopped more crime then cops!

I might have my first TK teammate.

CLICK

It's so many trolls that we'd be lucky to find someone who doesn't want to hurt them.

Let's find out who has suffered the most from social media trolling and I bet that's who is doing this.

I did find someone interesting....

This guy was a former Navy Seal and his daughter just overdosed after being bullied on social media.

That will give anyone a reason to get revenge.

is it enough to kill?

Send me his address. I'm going to pay Mr Saban a visit.

It's so many Trolls ! I think I'm going to need help.

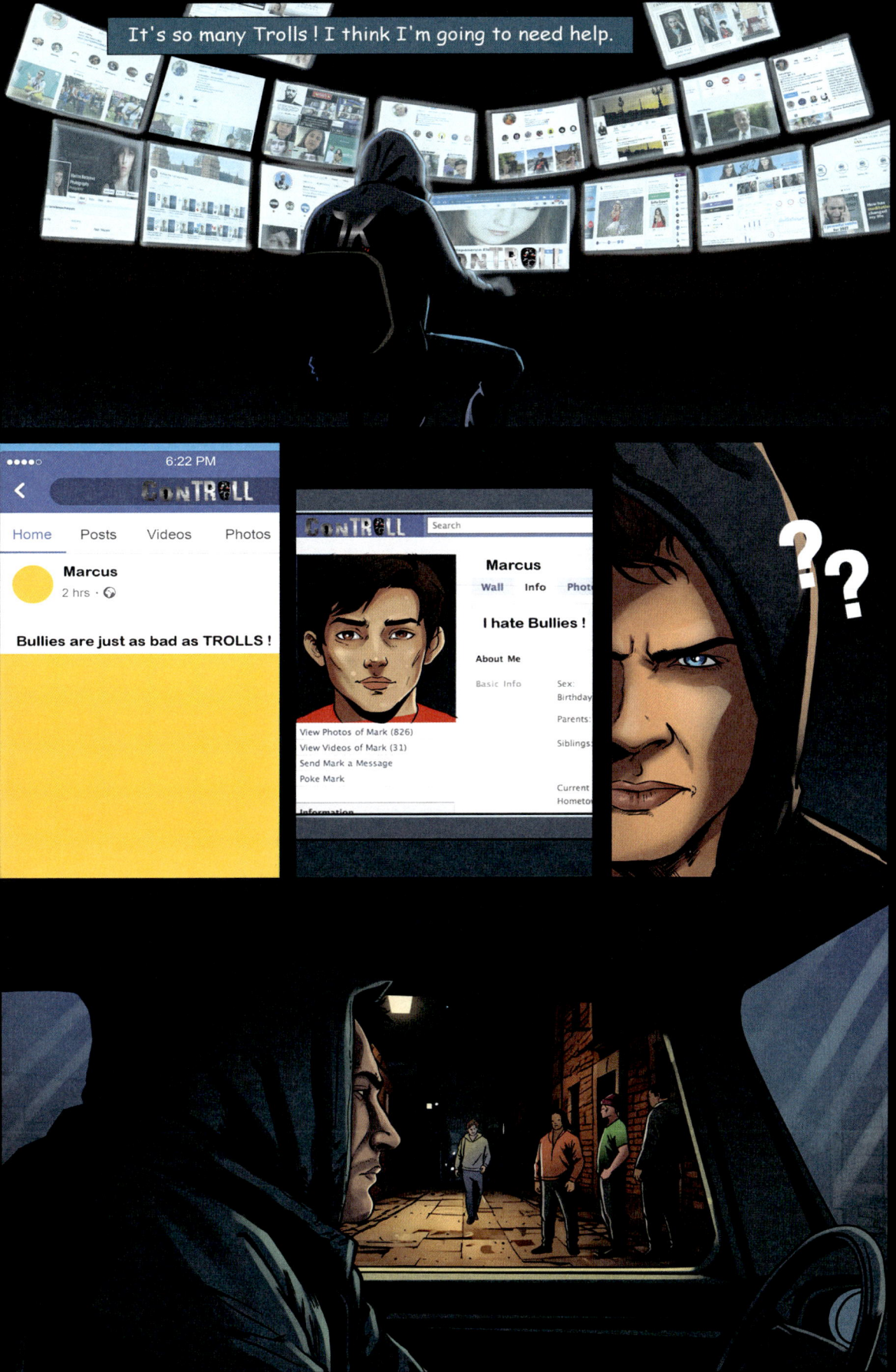

| Marcus walks past a group of street guys. | They all walk in front of him to stop him. |

| They mess with him by pointing a gun at him. | One of the thug punches him in the face while the other grabs his bag. |

They leave Marcus beaten and bleeding and walk away with his bag.

TK hates Bullies..

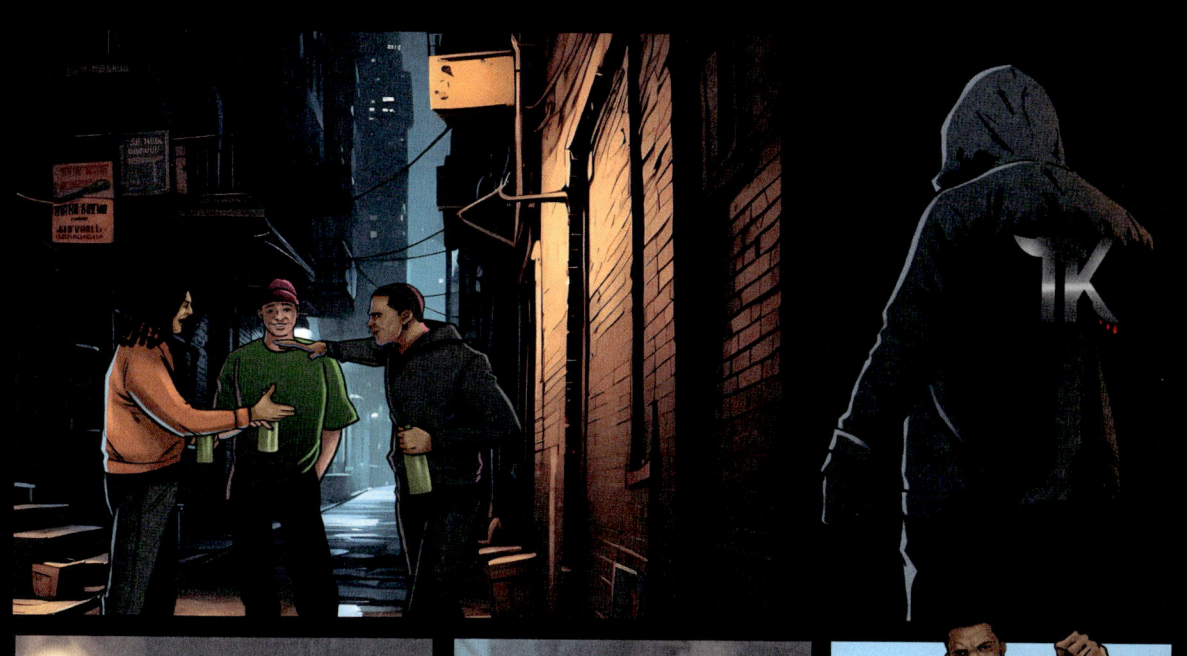

ARE YOU SABAN?
YOU WOULDN'T BE HERE IF I WASN'T.
CAN I COME IN AND TALK TO YOU?
I CAN HEAR YOU FROM MY DOORWAY.
THAT'S NOT HOW THIS WORKS.
IF YOU DON'T HAVE A WARRANT, THEN THAT'S HOW IT WORKS TODAY.
I KNOW WHO YOU ARE AND WHAT YOU'RE DOING. AND I WILL CATCH YOU.
YOU THINK YOU KNOW BUT YOU WILL FIND OUT SOON ENOUGH.

BAM..
BAM..
we have an image of TK in his mask.
It's time to relocate & create the ConTROLL ROOM.

Somewhere outside the City....
Can't let you cops stop my mission.
They want a fight.... But I want a WAR!
TK's Coming!

ConTROLL

TROLLS DON'T FEAR PEOPLE, THEY FEAR MONSTERS ~TK

CREATOR:
DEREK ANDERSON SR

TKinConTROLL

KARMA MISSED YOU TROLLS...BUT I WON'T

Made in the USA
Middletown, DE
17 January 2025